GEORGIA'S

ROME

GEORGIA'S
ROME
A BRIEF HISTORY

JERRY R. DESMOND

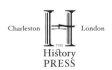

Charleston ——— London

THE
History
PRESS

Published by The History Press
Charleston, SC 29403
www.historypress.net

Cover design by Marshall Hudson.

All images courtesy of the Rome Area History Museum unless otherwise noted.

First published 2008

Manufactured in the United Kingdom

ISBN 978.1.59629.309.0

Library of Congress Cataloging-in-Publication Data

Desmond, Jerry R.
Georgia's Rome : a brief history / Jerry Desmond.
p. cm.
Includes bibliographical references.
ISBN 978-1-59629-309-0
1. Rome (Ga.)--History. I. Title.
F294.R7D47 2008
975.8'35--dc22

                    2008009385

Notice: The information in this book is true and complete to the best of our knowledge. It is offered without guarantee on the part of the author or The History Press. The author and The History Press disclaim all liability in connection with the use of this book.

CONTENTS

PREFACE

B efore being killed by the deadly fumes of Mount Vesuvius in AD 79 in an ill-advised attempt to get closer to have a "look-see," Pliny the Elder had established a reputation as Rome's most noted scientist, natural historian, philosopher and author. He is best known today for a few pithy quotes concerning human nature—"The only certainty is that nothing is certain," "The best plan is to profit from the folly of others" and "There is always something new out of Africa" are a few of his more insightful phrases. When we take a statement made by someone "with a grain of salt," we pay homage to Pliny Sr.'s wisdom. But the most famous quote from this ancient Roman applies directly to the nine generations of men and women who lived, worked and raised families in Georgia's Rome: "Home is where the heart is."

In fact, the residents of this relatively small city in northwest Georgia insist on taking the phrase a step further. We have been in our history and are now extremely proud of our community, almost to the point of (but not quite because it would be ungracious) arrogance. Were we shocked when *Forbes Magazine* ranked Rome as one of the best small places for business in the country in 2006? Not really. Were we surprised when the *New Rating Guide to Life in Small Cities*, published in 1997, picked Rome as the most livable small city in the Southeast? No, we already knew that. When we found out that our city school's students ranked number one in the state of Georgia on SAT scores in 2007 did we blush like a newly crowned beauty queen? Not even close. Are we amazed that our colleges and hospitals consistently place among the best in the country? The answer is evident.

This type of accomplishment and these awards are expected. These expectations echo from the distant past. When publisher Benjamin C. Yancy inserted his preface to the 1904 Rome City Directory, he wrote,

> *The splendid city of Rome is rising to her full stature to meet and embrace the opportunities that confront her. She is moving with steady and unfaltering step to the greater prosperity of the near future. Her foundations for success are as sure and immovable as the hills about her and on which she so proudly and firmly sits. Her people are intelligent, progressive and patriotic; her climate is uniform, temperate and delightful; her society is cultured, refined and hospitable; her health is well-nigh perfect; her schools are the best*

and her churches crown almost every hill. No city in the Southland can surpass her in manufacturing enterprises nor take rank above her in industrial pursuits.

Imagine then the near-arrogance of a four-year resident of the city in attempting to write a history of this great community. To add insult to injury, I was born and raised in the most northern area of Yankeedom—the state of Maine. (I have been repeatedly told that while anyone born in a Northern state is by definition a Yankee, a Damn Yankee is someone who visits the South and then stays.) In my defense, I can point to the fact that I am trained as a historian. As the executive director of the Rome Area History Museum, I come in daily contact with the history of the region, its people and its artifacts. It was only fitting that the editors of The History Press should look to the museum when considering an author for this work. I am, by default, that person and my heart is in the right place.

Furthermore, please remember this work is intended only as an introduction to the heritage and history of Rome, Georgia, and the surrounding area. It is accessible and illustrated with the hope of educating and entertaining the reader. It is basically a filtered retelling of the most popular stories of Rome's past, plus a few newer ones added in. It is not an in-depth study. For that, the history buff must go to one of several fine books on the subject. George Magruder Battey Jr.'s book, *A History of Rome and Floyd County*, self-published in 1922, runs for 640 pages. It contains a detailed account of Rome's early history, many anecdotes and reminiscences and a very valuable index of names. *All Roads to Rome*, by Roger Aycock, published in 1981 (dedicated to one of the founders of the Rome Area History Museum, Dr. C.J. Wyatt), is a wonderful narrative history of the region, running to 550 pages. Aycock's instincts as a newspaperman for finding the crux and twist in his stories are superb. In addition, *Rome and Floyd County, an Illustrated History* (1985), published by the Sesquicentennial Committee of the City of Rome, and *The Heritage of Floyd County, Georgia, 1833–1999* (1999), published by the Floyd County Heritage Book Committee, are invaluable resources for the historian.

Pliny the Elder of that other Rome also once wrote, "True glory consists in doing what deserves to be written; in writing what deserves to be read." It is a tall order for any historian. It implies some sort of mystical insight, combined with a grasp of the facts and an ability to tell a story. Barbara Tuchman, one of my favorite narrative historians, kept this reminder from one of her favorites, Catherine Drinker Bowen, above her writing desk: "Will the reader turn the page?" Let's find out. The hope is that it will at least be better than standing next to an active volcano.

ACKNOWLEDGEMENTS

The first decade of the twenty-first century saw the passing of a triumvirate of exceptional local historians in Rome, Georgia. Forrest Shropshire Sr., photographer, teacher and oral historian, died in 2003 at the age of eighty-eight; Roger D. Aycock, feature writer for the *Rome News-Tribune* and author of *All Roads to Rome*, died in 2004 at the age of eighty-nine; and Dr. C.J. Wyatt, one of the founders of the Rome Area History Museum, passed on in 2006 at the age of eighty-five (it is comforting to learn that historians seem to live long lives). Henceforth, all who study the history of the region, or attempt to write about it, owe a debt of gratitude to them for the passion for history that they demonstrated throughout their long careers. I did not have an opportunity to meet these remarkable men, but they cast long shadows and they will not be forgotten.

Russell McClanahan, on the other hand, is alive and well, working as the archivist at the Rome Area History Museum. His dedication to the preservation of Rome's history is matchless. To him I owe a debt of gratitude for pointing me in the right direction and finding several of the illustrations for this book previously hidden in the museum's archives. Kathy Grigsby, my administrative assistant at the museum, patiently listened as I bounced phrases and paragraphs at her, praising the effort whether I deserved it or not (as all administrative assistants should do).

The Board of Governors of the Rome Area History Museum must be commended for their volunteerism and vision for the future. Gardner Wright, chairman (great-great-grandson of one of the founders of Rome), and Janet Byington, president, are tireless in their promotion of Rome's museum. Their commitment is much appreciated. As is the commitment of those who went before them: Bobby McElwee, John Carruth (my Civil War buddy), Ed Byars, David Oswalt, Bernard Neal, Emily Saltino, Chip Tilly and others too numerous to mention.

My father, Jerry Desmond Sr., who passed away while this book was being written, could not have been more proud of his son than his son was proud of him. His love of history ignited a spark that will be paid forward.

My wife Cherry and my daughter Caroline are constant supporters and sources of inspiration. I hold them most dear.

CHAPTER ONE

CONQUISTADORS AND CHEROKEE

LAND BEFORE TIME

Let's go back 4.5 to 5 billion years. As Moses so succinctly put it, in the beginning the universe was created, galaxies sped outward and billions of stars and planets formed. On our planet, the outer crust began to cool during a 3.5-billion-year period known to scientists as the Precambrian Era. During this long stretch of time it began to rain. This was not just your average late afternoon shower. It rained for 100 million years, forming large bodies of water. Proteins and amino acids combined mysteriously in the warm water to form one-cell bacterias and sea plants. These blue-green algae multiplied and become larger, producing a byproduct that allowed life to expand to land areas—oxygen.

Over the next 400 million years, the variety of life increased dramatically. About 570 million years ago, during the Cambrian Period, hard shell sea creatures suddenly appeared in the cooling oceans. The surviving fossil record of this period gives us our first glimpse of life in the area that eventually became Georgia. As the continental plates drifted, North America collided with Africa and Europe, forming a giant continent known as Pangaea (Greek for "all land"). The pressure of this collision pushed upward a large mountain range that someday would be called the Appalachians, towering to forty thousand feet above the sea level. The northern part of this mountain range eventually split off again and became the highlands of Ireland and Scotland. (It is somehow poetic that the Scotch-Irish immigration to America in the seventeenth and eighteenth centuries occurred down a mountain range that actually started back in the old country.)

Life then became a little more complicated. Reptiles roamed the land during a period known as the Mesozoic or Middle Era. Because the land of northwest Georgia and northeast Alabama contained high mountains, this area has very little fossil record from the period. The thin air at an altitude ten thousand feet higher than Mount Everest would not have supported dinosaurs or any other type of animal life. However, the gradual erosion of the mountains over the next sixty-five million years and the rather sudden extinction of the dinosaurs resulted in the dawning of a new era—the Age of Mammals. Large rhinoceros-like creatures called brontotheres, saber-toothed tigers, mastodons and mammoths lived in the region. The fossil remains of the tapir, an insect-eating mammal now found in South America, have been uncovered in Walker and Bartow Counties. Huge black bears, giant ground sloths, extinct species of llamas and horses, jaguars and panthers also left fossil records of their existence. Then, sometime near the end of the last Ice Age, about twelve thousand years ago, a more dangerous mammal appeared—man.

NATIVES—WOODLAND AND MISSISSIPPIAN

As the giant glaciers of the last Ice Age melted, people who had crossed the land bridge between Siberia and Alaska, following the herds of mammoths and other game, became trapped by rising seas. However, a narrow corridor opened to the south, which both man and beast followed. Advancing with great speed, the descendants of these Siberian hunters may have reached the Atlantic Coast within five hundred years. Evidence suggests that Georgia had its first permanent settlers around 9,500 BC.

The next eight thousand years are called the Archaic Period. Settlers in the Southeast lived in small, family-based bands of between 50 and 150 people. They tended to migrate along the river systems of the region, following the game patterns, exhausting an area's food sources and then moving up or down the rivers to another location. They were hunters and gatherers; there is little or no evidence of agricultural activity in the early or middle Archaic Periods.

Hunters used large projectile points made of flint or chert on the ends of spears or darts. The spear thrower, or atlatl, was developed during this time. By increasing the speed that the spear could be thrown by use of this simple wooden lever, the hunter could increase his kill range and use fewer spears to accomplish a kill. It also made it possible for a hunter to kill faster animals like deer or more dangerous animals such as bears. This had the effect of increasing an area's food supply, resulting in a less mobile and larger population. The late Archaic Period also saw the development of pottery. Its appearance means that these people were now storing food, an advance that also suggests the development of agriculture.

The Woodland Period of native culture developed between 1,000 BC and AD 900, its name taken from the forests that covered North America at that time. An explosion in the technology of pottery, tools and weapons resulted in a more stable, sedentary lifestyle, although population pressures did result in some migrations. Ceramic cooking vessels appeared during the early Woodland Period. Pottery became more ornate. Fabric impressed, cord marked or stamped pottery did not just have visual appeal. The lines and carvings on the pottery made it easier to hold and less slippery. As the native potters learned to add sand and grit temper to the clay mixture instead of vegetable fiber, pots became more durable and larger. Large pots made it possible to store seasonal grains. Sumpweed was added to the list of domesticated plants, which included goosefoot, maygrass, knotweed and sunflower. Nuts, such as acorns, walnuts and hickory nuts, and other wild foods continued to form the bulk of the diet, however.

A great advance in hunting technology also occurred during the Woodland Period: hunters began using the bow and arrow. Several species of plants and some animal materials available in the Southeast met the requirements for making a bow. Ash, hickory, locust, Osage orange, cedar, juniper, oak, walnut, birch, chokecherry, serviceberry and mulberry woods were all used. Bowstrings were made from animal tendons, rawhide, gut or plant fibers. Arrow shafts were made out of shoots, such as dogwood, wild rose, ash, birch, chokecherry and black locust. The kill range made possible by the bow and arrow increased to two hundred yards, while the arrow shaft speed made it possible to kill large animals with a single shot.

Significant social change occurred during the middle Woodland Period (300 BC to AD 600). Forested areas were cleared, riverside settlements became more permanent and native populations grew larger. Social stratification and ritual ceremonialism also increased. The earliest earthen and rock mounds in Georgia date to this period. Most of these are small, dome-shaped structures that served as burial repositories. The earthen platform mounds also constructed during this time in Georgia probably functioned as stages for native rituals.

Since the Woodland natives were less mobile, trade between bands or tribes became necessary. For example, tribes in the northwestern section of Georgia, with abundant supplies of flint or chert, traded with coastal tribes who had shells. Exotic stones and copper from the Midwest were traded into this area. The most dramatic evidence of trade occurred by AD 200, when maize (corn) was introduced to the Southeast. Maize originated in Mexico and Central America. There are several theories concerning the actual route of the maize migration. It remains a mystery. However, the introduction of widespread maize cultivation marks the end of the Woodland Period.

The Mississippian Period of native culture lasted from AD 900 to AD 1600. Native settlements became more or less permanent. This permanence was a direct result of corn cultivation. It takes a village to grow this labor-intensive crop. It has to be planted, hilled, hoed and picked. It has to be husked, cleaned and the kernels have to be cut from the cob. The natives learned that beans and squash planted between the rows of corn protect the crop from insects and extreme temperature changes. These "three sisters" became the staples of the Mississippian diet. Game meats, fish, shellfish and turtles became protein supplements, along with nuts and fruits.

Because corn cultivation required that people live closer to each other and the fields, the Mississippians built shelters in which to live and store corn. These shelters were often round or rectangular, made by weaving saplings or cane around poles and then being covered with sun-baked clay. Roofs were covered with thatch, with a hole cut in the middle to allow smoke from the central fire to leave the structure. The settlement was often surrounded by a trench or pole wall to keep wild animals or other unwanted guests away from the stored food supply.

A consequence of the corn culture was the increase of conflict between neighboring groups. Crop failure in a region or chiefdom, caused by any number of factors—drought, insects, fire, hail, floods, etc.—increased the pressure to attack others to gain their supplies. In addition, in times of plenty, population pressures often demanded an increase in cultivation, causing further disputes among tribes.

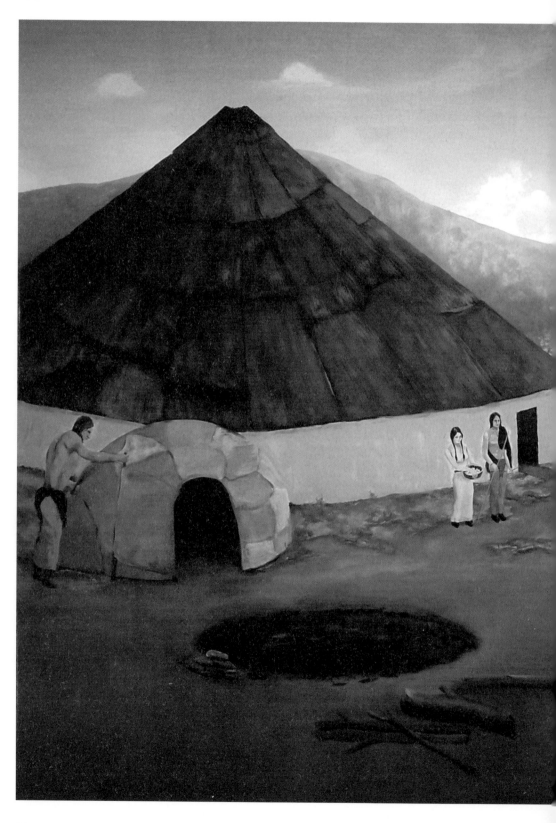

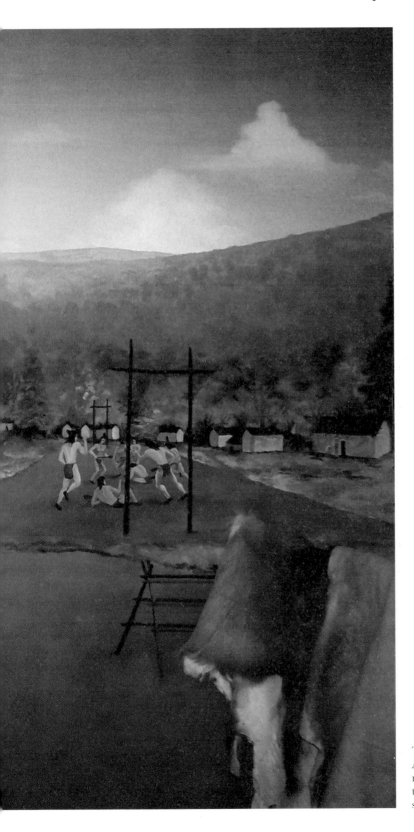

This wall mural at the Rome Area History Museum represents a native village in the period before European settlement.

All of this community building and protection required some sort of organization or government. Mississippian cultures were chiefdoms centered across Georgia's river valleys. In some of the larger settlements, great mounds were built, on which the chiefs conducted ceremonies, built their homes and in which they buried their ancestors. Eventually, near the end of the Mississippian Period, these chiefdoms could extend over hundreds of miles and include twenty to fifty villages. The paramount chiefdom of Coosa, for example, controlled at least seven smaller chiefdoms in the area that became northwest Georgia. For seven centuries, over thirty-five generations, Mississippian natives lived, raised families, worked, hunted and died. Then everything changed. Then came the Spanish.

DE SOTO

Nine states have towns named De Soto or DeSoto—Arkansas, Florida, Illinois, Indiana, Iowa, Kansas, Louisiana, Mississippi, Nebraska, Texas and Wisconsin. Several states have counties named for the Spanish explorer. There are quite a few DeSoto Parks, DeSoto Dams, DeSoto High Schools, DeSoto Shopping Malls and DeSoto Lakes. Maryland has DeSoto Road Business Park. Mississippi has DeSoto National Forest. Iowa has the DeSoto National Wildlife Refuge, near a curve in the Missouri River called the DeSoto Bend. Both Arizona and Nevada have the DeSoto Mines. Wisconsin has DeSoto Bay. Louisiana has the DeSoto Lookout Tower. Ohio has the DeSoto Historic Post Office. Minnesota has the DeSoto Trail (probably not one he ever used). In Rome, we have the DeSoto Theatre, DeSoto Park Baptist Church, DeSoto Beauty Shoppe and Tanning and a section of town that was once called DeSoto. Hundreds of small and large towns across the Southeast have impressive historical markers, statues and monuments proudly proclaiming that De Soto camped there, De Soto came through there, De Soto fought a battle there, etc. Heated academic controversies have stirred over the actual route that De Soto and his men took. Cities that were taken off the route in 1939 protested vigorously. Other places insist that he could have visited and invent scenarios to prove the point.

The question is, why? Hernando De Soto's travels through the Southeastern part of North America from 1539 to 1543 can only be described in terms of a natural disaster. One might as well name a town after a hurricane or an earthquake. Everywhere he and his men went they robbed, raped, pillaged, burned, took and killed hostages, tortured, fought battles and generally committed mayhem. The Mississippian towns and villages they left behind became leaderless, were stripped of food, infected with European viruses and partially or completely burned to the ground. Families were broken apart as De Soto's army kidnapped women and children to serve as slaves or pack animals. His visit destroyed a culture.

Hernando De Soto actually had prior experience with culture destruction. As a Spanish conquistador (conqueror), he joined Francisco Pizarro in his conquest of the Inca civilization in Peru in 1532. Returning to Spain a wealthy man, De Soto convinced

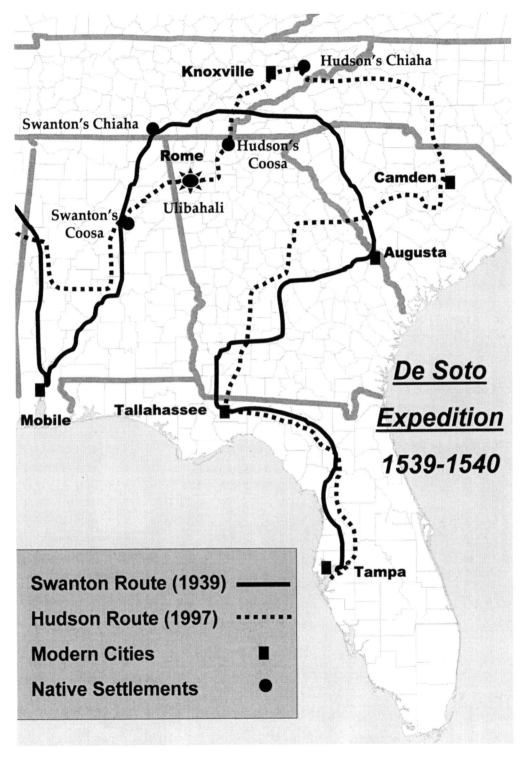

Two conflicting theories of De Soto's expedition route, 1539–40. *Map by the author.*

the King of Spain, Charles V, to let him return to the New World and begin an exploration of North America. In May of 1539, arriving on nine ships from Cuba, he landed near the present city of Tampa, Florida, with 620 men, 237 horses and 200 pigs (more on the pigs later). His goals, as with all Spanish explorations of this era, were to find passage to the Orient, discover sources of gold and establish colonies.

The exact route taken by De Soto's army has been in dispute almost from the day he set foot in Florida. In 1936, the United States Congress created a commission to discover De Soto's trail, to be published at the four hundredth anniversary of his landing. Dr. John R. Swanton, a Harvard ethnologist, was appointed to chair that committee, which also consisted of congressmen from six Southern states. Ignoring at least ten previous studies of the route, Swanton, under some political pressure, published an official route unlike any other. Markers were placed along the trail, stamped with a seal of approval from the U.S. government.

For northwest Georgia, the Swanton Report was another De Soto disaster. Swanton had the Spanish completely sidestep the region, placing the all-important settlement of Coosa in Talladega County, Alabama. The settlement of Chiaha, long considered to be somewhere near or in Floyd County, was moved near Chattanooga, Tennessee. Festivals to "celebrate" De Soto were canceled and the matter was forgotten for nearly thirty years.

Then, in the mid-1970s, the study of the route regained some steam. An earlier excavation of Swanton's proposed Coosa settlement in 1948 found that the site was more likely a village typical of the mid-1700s, two hundred years after De Soto's expedition. Scholars began to wonder, if Swanton had been wrong about Coosa, why not some of the other settlements? In 1982, two natives of Floyd County and a friend from Alabama, while trespassing on a farm near an archaeological dig along the Coosa River known as the King Site, found a Spanish sword. While this did not prove that De Soto had visited Floyd County (it could have been left by a later expedition headed by Tristan de Luna in 1560), it did reopen the possibility. Finally, in the 1990s, Dr. Charles Hudson published the findings of twenty years of study in a book entitled *Knights of Spain, Warriors of the Sun: Hernando de Soto and the South's Ancient Chiefdoms*. It seemed to lay to rest the route controversy. While Hudson does not put either Coosa or Chiaha anywhere near Rome, he does have De Soto visiting the future site of the city on August 31, 1540.

Fully a year into his travels, De Soto's army moved from the present site of the Etowah Indian Mounds in Cartersville, Georgia, along the Etowah River to the native village of Ulibahali, at the confluence of the Etowah and Oostanaula Rivers. Based on the accounts of two of De Soto's men, they camped for several days (probably at the present site of the tennis courts of the Coosa Valley County Club). Holding Chief Coosa hostage, De Soto entered Ulibahali to find the natives very upset with the handling of their supreme chief from the north. Chief Coosa, who had greeted the Spanish warmly in July only to become a captive, requested that they lay down their weapons. The situation was defused. De Soto demanded and received twenty women as slaves, leaving the village on September 2, 1540, to continue down the Coosa River Valley into present-day Alabama.

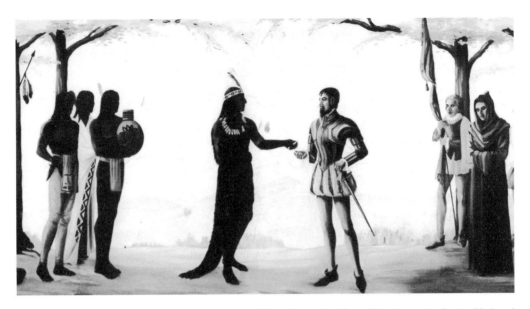

In 1935, Margaret Bryson, a local artist, was commissioned to paint three historic murals for the National City Bank (now Wachovia) on Broad Street. This mural depicts the visit of Hernando De Soto to the area in 1540.

As word spread of the harsh treatment meted out by the Spanish, natives in their path soon either fled or turned to resistance. Several running battles were fought as De Soto ranged across northern Alabama and Mississippi. Eventually reaching the Mississippi River, which he crossed with his remaining four hundred men, he died of a fever on the opposite bank in 1542. After many hardships, the remnants of his expedition staggered into Mexico in 1543.

While the De Soto expedition must be classified a failure, the long-term results for native populations in their path could only be called catastrophic. Entire populations were wiped out by diseases such as smallpox and measles. The introduction of pigs into the Southeast had dire ecological consequences. With their ability to double their population every four months, the pigs left behind by the Spanish soon were destroying crops and rooting out forests across the area. By 1600, the entire culture had collapsed, creating a vacuum into which a new group from the North, who called themselves the Ani-Yunwiya, or the principal people, would rush.

CHEROKEE

There are several theories about the meaning of the name Cherokee. The Cherokee language is markedly different from other native languages in the Southeast. Thus, a Creek word "chilakee," meaning "people of a different speech," seems a reasonable source for the name. There is some evidence that the Cherokee at one time lived in the upper valleys of the Ohio River just south of the Iroquois, whose language is most like their own. As the Cherokee were pushed south by the expansion of the Iroquois and Delaware, they moved into the central Appalachians. By the early 1600s, the Cherokee roamed over an area that extended from western Virginia to western South Carolina and eastern Tennessee. Their location in the interior mountains kept them isolated for much of the seventeenth century, although contact with English traders began as early as 1629.

This does not mean that the 1600s were uneventful. At one time or another, the Cherokee fought territorial wars with the Iroquois, the Catabaw, the Creek, the Choctaw, the Shawnee and the Chickasaw, with mixed results. The British inserted themselves more and more into the complicated picture as settlers began expanding from the coastal areas of North and South Carolina. The introduction of firearms in the late seventeenth century did nothing to lesson tensions. In 1715, the Cherokee participated in a general uprising against the Carolinas that eventually resulted in a treaty being signed in 1721. It established a boundary between the Cherokee and British settlements, regulated trade and confirmed an alliance that lasted for the rest of the century. It ominously was also the first land cession made by the Cherokee. In 1738 and 1753, smallpox outbreaks resulted in the death of at least a quarter of the Cherokee population, which had been estimated to be as high as twenty thousand in 1729.

To compensate for growing losses to white settlement, the Cherokee moved into northern Georgia, a territory formerly shared with the Creek. In 1755, the decisive Battle of Taliwa occurred near the present-day town of Ball Ground in Cherokee County. Outnumbered four to one, five hundred Cherokee, led by Chief Oconostota, held off five charges by the Creek warriors. On the fifth charge, a Cherokee warrior named Kingfisher was killed. His wife, Nancy Ward, took up his weapon and led the Cherokee to victory. For this act of courage she was named ghighua, or "beloved woman," of the Cherokee nation. She was allowed to sit in tribal councils and make decisions on pardons. Except for a small village near Rome, the Creek ceded all lands north of the Chattahoochee River to the Cherokee.

After changing sides several times during the French and Indian War of 1755–63, the Cherokee again attempted to compensate for losses to English settlers by moving against a neighboring tribe. But their intended victim, the Chickasaw, were too powerful. After eleven years, the Cherokee gave up. This was followed by a strategy of ceding lands already taken from them and selling lands they did not control. For example, in 1775 they sold all of eastern and central Kentucky to the Transylvania Land Company, although much of this area was Shawnee territory. At the conclusion of the Transylvania Treaty of 1775, the great Cherokee warrior Dragging Canoe spoke against the sale of further land:

> *Whole Indian nations have melted away like snowballs in the sun before the white man's advance. They leave scarcely a name of our people except those wrongly recorded by their destroyers. Where are the Delawares? They have been reduced to a mere shadow of their former greatness. We had hoped that the white men would not be willing to travel beyond the mountains. Now that hope is gone. They have passed the mountains, and have settled*

upon Cherokee land. They wish to have that action sanctioned by treaty. When that is gained, the same encroaching spirit will lead them upon other land of the Cherokees. New cessions will be asked. Finally the whole country, which the Cherokees and their fathers have so long occupied, will be demanded, and the remnant of Ani-Yunwiya, the real people, once so great and formidable, will be compelled to seek refuge in some distant wilderness. There they will be permitted to stay only a short while, until they again behold the advancing banners of the same greedy host. Not being able to point out any further retreat for the miserable Cherokees, the extinction of the whole race will be proclaimed. Should we not therefore run all risks, and incur all consequences, rather than submit to further loss of our country? Such treaties may be alright for men who are too old to hunt or fight. As for me, I have my young warriors about me. We will have our lands. A-WANINSKI, I have spoken.

Prophetic words indeed! Dragging Canoe and the Chickamauga band of the Cherokee sided with the British during the American Revolution. The British policy of giving bounties for scalps ("horses and hair") led to several atrocities along the frontier. When the Chickamauga attacked two American forts in 1776, the American militia, unable or unwilling to distinguish between hostile and neutral Cherokee, destroyed more than thirty-six Cherokee towns. The Cherokee sued for peace, finally ceding almost all of their lands in the Carolinas at the Treaty of Hopewell in 1786. The Chickamauga, however, fought on even after Dragging Canoe's death in 1792.

THE BATTLE OF ETOWAH

The battle that many historians believe finally broke the back of Cherokee resistance occurred at the foot of Myrtle Hill in 1793. Seeking blood vengeance for an earlier massacre, Cherokee Chief John Watts, with about seven hundred Creek and three hundred Cherokee warriors, led a raid into northeastern Tennessee. In the group were Doublehead, the notorious Cherokee leader; Kah-nung-da-tla-geh (later known as Major Ridge), the young grandson of Oconostota; and James Vann. Diverting away from a heavily defended Knoxville, the party attacked a blockhouse known as Cavett's Station about eight miles to the west of the town. The sixteen men, women and children in the blockhouse surrendered after being told their lives would be spared and promised that they would be exchanged for native prisoners. However, Doublehead and his followers did not agree to the truce and begin killing the members of Cavett's family. James Vann attempted to protect one young boy by hoisting him on his saddle, but Doublehead rushed at the boy and killed him with a single blow to the head (thereafter, Vann's allies called Doublehead "kill baby"). With very little to show for the raid, they returned to Georgia.

Meanwhile, under orders from William Blount, provisional governor of the Tennessee territory, General John Sevier, leading about seven hundred volunteer militiamen, rushed south to punish those involved in the Cavett's Station massacre. Sevier, called Nolichucky Jack for his exploits along the Nolichucky River, was known as a ruthless Indian fighter with

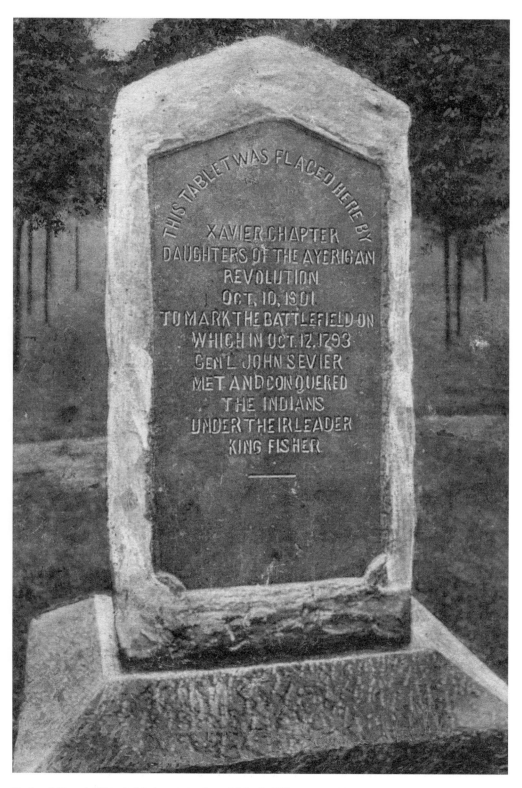

Battle of Etowah Historic Marker at the foot of Myrtle Hill.

no tendency toward mercy. Burning towns as he moved south, Sevier reached Ustanali, a few miles from present-day Calhoun. Finding the town deserted, he burned it and divided his small army, sending some companies down the Etowah River while moving down the Oostanaula with the rest of his force. He hoped to catch the main force of Cherokee and Creek at Hightower (also known as Old Coosa Town or Etowah Town). On October 17, 1793, the Battle of Etowah (also called the Battle of Hightower) was fought.

Learning of the approach of their mortal enemy, Nolichucky Jack, the Cherokee and Creek under Chief King Fisher had taken a strong position at the foot of a rocky bluff (known now as Myrtle Hill) across the Etowah River. He had extended his line to guard a ford across the river. Finding that the militia were attempting to cross the river about a half mile below the ford, the Cherokee and Creek abandoned their strongly fortified position and rushed to the spot, only to discover that the militia had instead moved on to the ford. The engagement at the ford was brief but violent. A young Tennessee militiaman named Hugh Lawson White (later senator from Tennessee and presidential candidate in 1836) shot King Fisher in the chest. The remaining warriors fled following the death of their leader. With only three men killed and four men wounded (along with two or three horses killed), John Sevier's last military campaign came to a close.

CHEROKEE REMOVAL

The next forty years, between 1792 and 1832, witnessed the remarkable transformation of the Cherokee from a warlike tribe to a "civilized" nation. The Indian policy of the United States under President Washington (1789–1797) could be described as a mixed bag. North of the Ohio River, the policy was one of extermination and removal. In the Southeast, Washington, perhaps due to personal memories of Cherokee friendship during the French and Indian War, followed a policy of assimilation. Basically this policy included the protection of Indian rights to land, the setting of boundaries and controlling settlers' access and encroachment on Indian lands. Attempts were made to regulate trade with Indians, to control the traffic of liquor and to provide for dealing with crimes committed by whites or Indians against each other to eliminate vigilantism. The main thrust, however, involved an effort to civilize and educate the natives in the ways of the white man. In 1791, for example, the Treaty of Holston involved a cession of Cherokee land in eastern Tennessee in exchange for President Washington's guarantee that the Cherokee would never again be invaded by settlers. It gave the Cherokee the right to evict settlers in their territory and required Americans to obtain passports to enter Cherokee lands.

In 1794, a group of Cherokee leaders visited Philadelphia to meet with President Washington. Even the infamous Doublehead attended the meetings, going so far as to appoint himself spokesman for the delegation. (It is reported that Doublehead played up his reputation as a bloodthirsty savage while in Philadelphia, dressing in elaborate costumes and making outrageous statements. When one reporter asked him his opinion of the white race, he replied without hesitation, "Too salty.") However, the good relations between the American government and the Cherokee barely survived Washington's administration. In 1802, President Jefferson formally promised all Cherokee lands within its boundaries to the state of Georgia. Thereafter, Georgia refused to recognize the Cherokee Nation or its land claims.

Meanwhile, Doublehead, having given up his murderous ways, under the protection of the U.S. government and with a $5,000 a year annuity, settled into a new lifestyle. Suddenly becoming quite wealthy (rumors spread that he had found a cave with bags of silver coins hidden by De Soto), Doublehead made trips to New Orleans, Charleston and even New York (where, as a typical tourist, he took in a play). He did, however, resist the movement toward total acceptance of the white man's ways, regretting the loss of Cherokee customs. This brought him into direct conflict with a group of younger chiefs in council who favored assimilation. The final straw occurred in 1806, when Doublehead and Indian agent Colonel Return J. Meigs arraigned for the cession of almost ten million acres of Cherokee land. The Blood Law of the Cherokee Nation called for the execution of anyone selling lands without the Nation's approval.

James Vann, Alexander Saunders and Major Ridge were selected to perform the deed. However, on the way to Hiawasee, Vann fell ill (drunk), leaving the job to Saunders and Ridge. Waiting in ambush at MacIntosh's tavern, Ridge shot Doublehead in the jaw. Thinking he was dead, Ridge and Saunders quickly slipped from the tavern, only to learn the next day that Doublehead had survived. Finding his hiding place, Doublehead, his jaw shattered, rushed at Ridge, grappling with him until Saunders shot him in the hip. Saunders then drove his tomahawk into the chief's forehead, finishing the job.

The new mixed-blood leadership of Vann, Ridge and John Ross soon began introducing major cultural changes. To ensure that there would be no reprisals for the assassination of Doublehead, Ridge, who had built a beautiful home on the Oostanaula River near present-day Rome (now the Chieftains Museum), pushed for the repeal of the Blood Law. Almost overnight, the Cherokee assumed the ways of the white man. In 1817, the clan system of government was replaced with an elected tribal council. The capital was moved to New Echota in 1825 and the Cherokee adopted a written constitution based on the American model.

In 1821, Sequoyah (also known as George Gist, the nephew of Doublehead) invented the Cherokee alphabet. Soon thousands of Cherokee were reading the *Cherokee Phoenix*, a newspaper in their own language. Many became prosperous farmers. Chief John Ross, for example, had a house valued at $10,000 designed by a Philadelphia architect. A census taken in 1826 found that the Cherokee owned 1,560 black slaves, 22,000 cattle, 7,600 horses, 2,942 plows and 46,000 pigs. They operated 762 looms, owned 2,488 spinning wheels, 10 sawmills, 31 gristmills, 62 blacksmith shops, 18 schools and 18 ferries.

To accommodate their new allies, the Cherokee rejected the great Shawnee Chief Tecumseh's overtures to form an Indian Confederacy against the Americans in 1811. They instead joined General Andrew Jackson's army during the Creek War of 1813–14. At the Battle of Horseshoe Bend, Ridge, who had organized a force of eight hundred warriors, was in the first canoe to cross the Tallapoosa River to attack the Creek rear. After the victory, he was given the rank of major for his bravery, a title he carried to

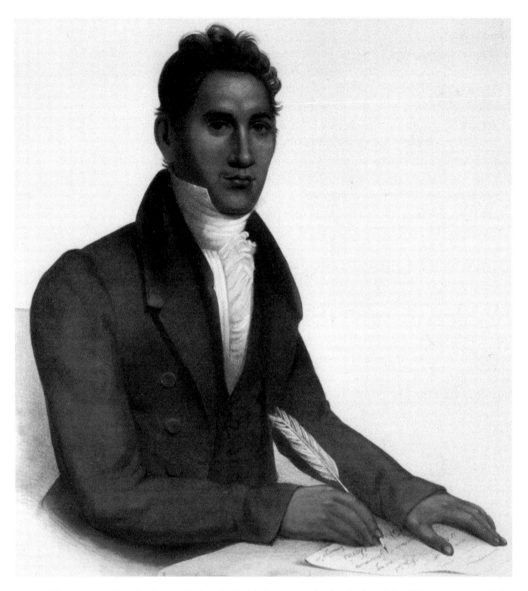

John Ridge portrait by Charles Bird King (1826). The son of Major Ridge, John Ridge was one of the signers of the Treaty of New Echota. *Courtesy of the Smithsonian Institution.*

the end of his life. The Cherokee were then stunned when Jackson (who reportedly had been saved at the battle by a Cherokee warrior) demanded huge land cessions at the end of the war.

The election of Andrew Jackson as president in 1828 and the discovery of gold in Cherokee territory that same year marked the beginning of the end of the Cherokee in Georgia. Facing political pressure and with a firm belief that whites and Indians could not live together, Jackson signed the Indian Removal Act in 1830. The state of Georgia immediately began dividing up Cherokee lands by lottery, stripping the Cherokee of legal protections and extending its laws into the territory. Chief John Ross decided to bring the fight to the United States Supreme Court. In two landmark decisions, Chief Justice John Marshall sided with the Cherokee, recognizing their sovereign status. In a famous reply, President Jackson answered, "John Marshall has made his decision, now let him enforce it."

Realizing the hopelessness of the situation and wishing to avoid genocide, a group led by Major Ridge; his son, John Ridge; Elias Boudinot, the editor of the *Phoenix*; and others signed the Treaty of New Echota in December of 1835. The treaty surrendered the Cherokee homeland in exchange for $5 million, seven million acres of land in the Indian Territory (Oklahoma) and an agreement to remove within two years. Only 350 of the estimated 17,000 Cherokee actually signed the treaty. John Ross then sent a petition signed by 16,000 Cherokee rejecting the treaty to the U.S. Senate, but after a violent debate the treaty passed by one vote.

When the deadline for removal arrived in May of 1838, General Winfield Scott, with seven thousand soldiers, moved into Cherokee territory to round up those who had not already moved west. Some were brought to concentration camps near Chattanooga, where unsanitary conditions led to the death of many. It is estimated that four thousand Cherokee died en route to Oklahoma, including the wife of John Ross. Embittered by his loss, John Ross ordered the assassination of Major Ridge, John Ridge, Elias Boudinot and others. On June 22, 1839, John Ridge was stabbed twenty-five times in front of his family; his father and Boudinot were also murdered on that day. While a few Cherokee managed to escape to the mountains of North and South Carolina, the Cherokee presence in northwest Georgia came to an end.

CHAPTER TWO

A PICTURESQUE PLACE

THE FOUNDING OF ROME

The sale of public lands in the state of Georgia has always been controversial. Following independence from England, the state adopted a headright system, allowing the governor to give grants of land, a power formerly held by the English monarch. As an incentive to bring settlers to the state, each "head" of a family could be granted two hundred acres plus fifty acres for each additional family member, up to one thousand acres. Due to substantial fraud (many friends of the Executive Council received more than one thousand acres), the power was eventually transferred to land courts in each county. However, in 1795 the Georgia Assembly passed the Yazoo Land Act, selling forty million acres of public lands claimed by Georgia in present-day Alabama and Mississippi to several land companies for $500,000, or $1\frac{1}{4}$ cents per acre. When it was discovered that a number of the assemblymen were shareholders in these companies, the public outcry was great, resulting in a major upheaval in Georgia politics. The Yazoo Land Act was repealed and money was returned, although some of the land had already been resold to investors who preferred to keep the land rather than accept a refund. The state then refused to recognize their claims, which led to a decade of countersuits and court rulings.

To avoid further fraud, the State Assembly decided to try a new system of land distribution. Between 1805 and 1833, the state conducted eight land lotteries (Georgia became the only state in the country to use a lottery system to distribute land). The first five lotteries—held in 1805, 1807, 1820, 1821 and 1827—distributed lands formerly held by the Creek Indians in the state. In 1832, two lotteries were held to divide Cherokee lands. In the sixth lottery, 85,000 people competed for 18,309 land lots of 160 acres each. Tickets with the name of the participants were placed in a barrel drum, while another drum held the lot locations. Additional empty tickets were put in the second drum to compensate for the oversubscription. "Fortunate drawers" were then only required to pay an eighteen-dollar fee for the lot. The seventh lottery, also held in 1832, known as the "Gold Lottery," was for special 40-acre lots that the state felt might have gold deposits (although no guarantees were given). Over 133,000 people participated in

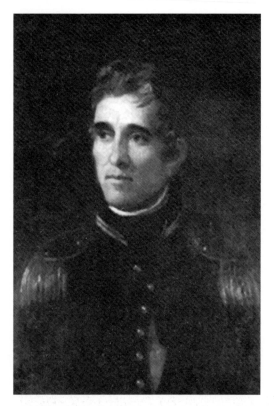

Floyd County was named in honor of General John Floyd, noted Indian fighter.

this lottery for 35,000 gold belt lots. A final, eighth lottery held in 1833 distributed lots and fractions from the 1832 Land Lottery and from the 1832 Gold Lottery not placed in the prize wheels during those lotteries.

On December 3, 1832, the state of Georgia passed an act dividing the Cherokee lands into ten large counties (eventually these counties were further divided into twenty-nine smaller counties). In this district, Floyd County was named for General John Floyd, Indian fighter and hero of the Creek wars. It was considered to be one of the finer sections of Cherokee land. Both John Ross and Major Ridge had homes in the district. The transfer of ownership of these lands from Cherokee to white settlers resulted in heightened tensions in the region. A census conducted by the state of Georgia in 1835 showed that 1,120 mixed-blood and full-blood Cherokee and their slaves still lived in Floyd County. In 1833, the land was surveyed by Jacob M. Scudder. The tiny town of Livingston, a few miles upstream from the head of the Coosa River, became the first county seat.

The story of Rome's founding has passed into legend. In the spring of 1834, Colonel Daniel R. Mitchell, a lawyer from Canton, and Colonel Zachariah B. Hargrove, a lawyer from Cassville, were traveling to attend court at the county seat in Livingston. They stopped at a spring (now trapped below Broad Street and East Third Avenue) to water their horses. As they sat and rested under a willow tree, they noted the beautiful scenery of the area and the availability of water, thinking it would be a wonderful

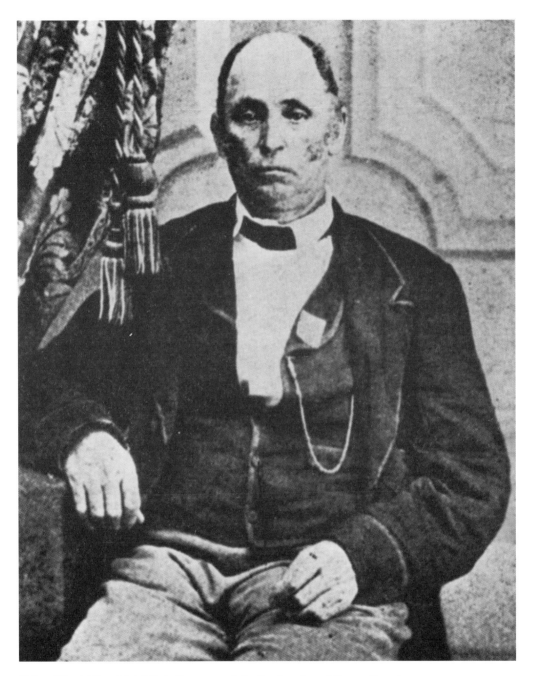

Colonel Daniel Randolph Mitchell was one of the five founders of Rome, Georgia.

place to build a town. Another gentleman stopped at the spring. Overhearing their conversation, he introduced himself as Major Philip Walker Hemphill (at this point, one must wonder if there was anyone under the rank of captain in the area). He invited them to spend the night at his home to further discuss the possibilities. Taking the Forks Ferry, owned by John Ross, they traveled a mile or so to Hemphill's mansion, Alhambra (now the headmaster's home on the Darlington school campus). The next day, following the court session, they spent another night at Hemphill's home, meeting another colonel, William Smith from Cave Spring. The men quickly agreed to buy all available land situated in the peninsula formed by the coming together of the Etowah and Oostanaula Rivers, plus the rights to operate the ferry. It was further agreed that a fifth member, John H. Lumpkin (no apparent military rank), the nephew of Georgia Governor Wilson Lumpkin, be added to the group in an effort to move the county seat from Livingston to the new town.

The only matter left to be settled was naming the new enterprise. In true lottery form, the men each agreed to put a name on a piece of paper into a hat. Smith suggested Hillsboro for the rolling hills in the area. Hemphill, believing the town might one day become a great commercial city, suggested Hamburg, after the city on the Elbe River in Germany. Lumpkin preferred Warsaw, after the great Polish city. Mitchell, reminded of seven hills along the Tiber River in Italy, thought Rome was a grand enough name. Hargrove, perhaps being less cosmopolitan, thought Pittsburgh appropriate. Mitchell was given the honor of drawing the name from the hat (whether he peeked or not is part of the legend). Rome it was.

THREE RIVERS AND SEVEN HILLS

The five founders certainly had an eye for real estate, as the town quickly developed and prospered, meeting their best expectations. Of prime importance was its strategic location on three rivers. The Etowah, from the Creek word "Eltawa," meaning "trail crossing," flows generally west-southwest 160 miles from its source near Dahlonega, Georgia. Earlier maps of the region occasionally labeled it Hightower River. The Oostanaula River forms in northern Gordon County at the confluence of the Conasauga and Coosawattee Rivers. It flows south-southwestwardly through Gordon and Floyd Counties, past the towns of Resaca and Calhoun. It has been spelled Estanola, Oostenauleh, Oustanalee and even Ustanali on maps of the region, the Cherokee translation meaning "rock that bars the way." It joins the Etowah River at Rome to form the Coosa River. The Coosa River then flows westward into Alabama, shifting south, joining the Tallapoosa River to form the Alabama River, which then flows down to Mobile Bay and the Gulf of Mexico. All three rivers are navigable, although several shoals and waterfalls required portage or "mule hauling."

The neck of land between the rivers was heavily wooded in 1834. Like its namesake in Italy, Rome has seven hills that gently contribute to its eye pleasing contours. In South Rome, Mount Aventine, the only hill with an ancient name, and Myrtle Hill form a barrier that forces the Etowah River to make a sweeping turn to the north before meeting the Oostanaula River. In downtown historic Rome, three hills dominate the city: Old Shorter Hill, once the site of Shorter College; Tower Hill, on whose peak the clock tower rests; and Lumpkin Hill, named for one of the five founders. Finally, in North Rome, Blossom Hill, the present location of the Rome Visitors Center, and Fort Jackson Hill, the site of a Civil War fort, complete the septet. (Note: a visitor to Rome today or a new resident must surely find the geographical section names for the city to be confusing. South Rome, by the compass, lies to the west; East Rome is south of the Etowah River; West Rome is actually more north; and North Rome is, at best, to the northeast of downtown historic Rome.)

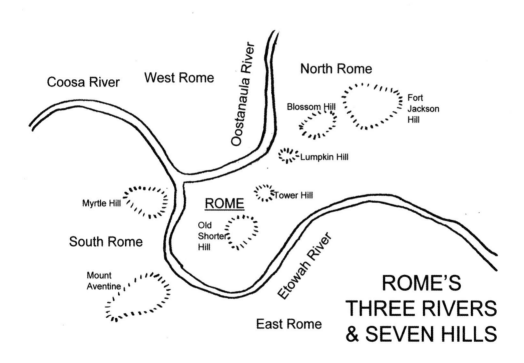

Rome's three rivers and seven hills. *Map by the author.*

Colonel Mitchell wasted no time, after the establishment of the town, in plotting out the town streets and lots. Using a Gunter 's chain, an old surveyor's measuring device made of one hundred links of wire exactly 66 feet long attached to four poles, Mitchell decided that the streets needed to be one chain wide. Lanes and lesser streets would be half a chain wide, or 33 feet. The main street extending down the peninsula he made two chains wide, or 132 feet. It was called Broad Street; the other avenues and streets were numbered and criss-crossed according to the custom of the period. The area closest to the confluence of the rivers, owned by Colonel Smith, was not plotted, as it generally flooded in the spring. He built a half-mile racetrack on the property and held horse races there for many years.

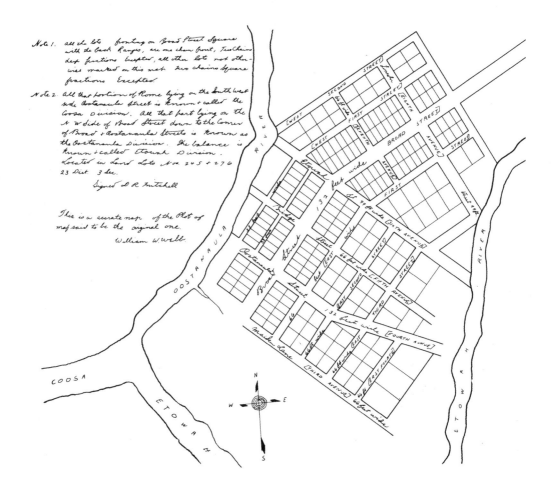

The city of Rome as laid out by D.R. Mitchell in 1834.

GROWTH AND GROWING PAINS

It would be a fabrication to report that the first settlers in the new town were all churchgoing, law-abiding citizens. For a period of time, Rome experienced a rough and tumble time as chaotic as any frontier town in the Wild West. Tension existed between the newcomers and the remaining Cherokee. Fraudulent land claims led to bitter disputes, mysterious fires and occassional violence. For every church built in town, there were three or four saloons. The town took a while to settle down. Much of the credit for the eventual cooling must go to Colonels Mitchell and Smith. Daniel Mitchell organized the Rome Bar with John Lumpkin and others, practicing law for many years. He helped to raise funds to build the courthouse after the county seat was moved from Livingston. Colonel William Smith had his hands full as the first county sheriff. All of the founding fathers had multiple interests and businesses in town.

The great value of George M. Battey Jr.'s book, *A History of Rome and Floyd County*, is the impressive number of family names and "firsts" he lists from Rome's earliest times. The first bank in Rome was the Western Bank of Georgia, with William C. Hardin as president. The first church, founded in May of 1835, was the First Baptist Church (the First Presbyterian Church was founded in Livingston in 1833 but only moved to Rome in 1845). The first inn, kept by William Quinn, was Cross Keys, at the junction of several streets now known as Five Points. The first newspaper was the *Western Georgian*, published by J. Hemphill and S. Jack in 1837. These firsts were followed by seconds, thirds and fourths in many cases. For example, perhaps the finest hotel in early Rome was the Choice House, built by John Choice sometime before 1850. It was located at the corner of Fifth Avenue and Broad Street, later to become the location of the Hotel General Forrest. The Buena Vista Hotel, a brick building built on Sixth Avenue in 1843, had an Irish proprietor, Thomas Burke (later in financial trouble, Burke transferred the property to Daniel Mitchell in payment for legal services). Other hotels included the Etowah House on East Second Avenue and the Tennessee House. The Methodists built a church in 1840, on land donated by Daniel Mitchell, with St. Peter's Episcopal Church coming later in 1854.

With the almost frantic building of hotels, churches, saloons, stables, dry goods stores and homes, the lumber business boomed. Flatboats carrying fresh-cut logs crowded the rivers on a daily basis, much of the work being done by black slaves. (Note: When historians of the period write, for example, that Colonel Mitchell built a house on West Eleventh Street, the reader must insert a mental edit—Colonel Mitchell, in fact, supervised the building of a house by his slaves. Rome was not built in a day, but a great deal of it was built with slave labor.)

As the town began filling up, lot prices rose dramatically. Early on, some lots were going for as little as $10, but soon the price ballooned to $110 and then jumped again to the $300 to $500 range. Unfortunately, the streets and roads in town did not match the impressive buildings going up. At best just dusty and crowded with roaming cows and pigs, the roads during the rainy season became vast quagmires of mud, the effect multiplied by the sloping nature of the ground. It would take seventy-five years before the road situation improved much. Stagecoaches did run three times a week to New

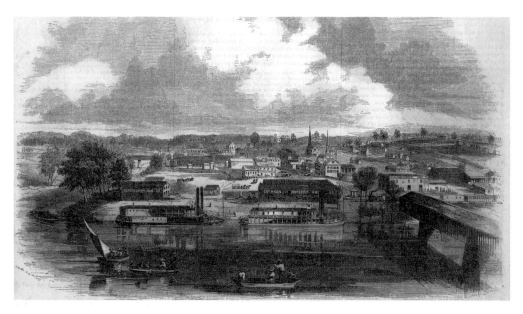

"View of Rome, Georgia," published by *Ballou's Pictorial* on November 1, 1856.

Echota, Cave Spring and Jacksonville, Alabama. Eventually connections were made with Athens, Milledgeville, Macon and Augusta. The stage brought mail to a post office that was set up in the center of town.

By 1850, after only fifteen years, the town had a population approaching 2,500, with an additional 5,700 citizens living in the surrounding areas of Floyd County. Incorporated as a city in 1847, Rome had a volunteer fire department, street lamps, a jewelry store, four drugstores, three livery stables, a college for females, a bookstore, a host of lawyers and doctors (56 by 1860), a number of grocery stores and a railroad connection to the outside world. In November of 1856, the front page of *Ballou's Pictorial*, a popular illustrated newspaper published in Boston, Massachusetts, featured a lithograph of the city and an editorial lavishly praising the area:

> *We present on this page a fine engraving, from a drawing by Hill, reduced from a most elaborate delineation made for us by Mr. A. Grinevald* [an artist from Charleston, South Carolina], *on the spot. It represents faithfully the flourishing city of Rome, the capital of Floyd County, Georgia, which is situated at the confluence of the Etowah and Oostenaula rivers, forming the Coosa. It is 170 miles northwest of Milledgeville. Its site, embracing several hills, affords an extensive view of some of the finest scenery in the State…The situation of Rome is certainly very romantic and the buildings of which it is composed are neat, pretty and unostentatious. No matter how crowded it becomes, it will always be a picturesque place. The streets are laid out of a liberal width, permitting a free circulation of air, and allowing ample accommodation for present and prospective travel…The settlers of villiages in these days look to see them grow into large towns, and from large towns to large cities, and are therefore ready to meet coming contingencies.*

STEAM

Today it would be hard to imagine the excitement and awe caused by the appearance of a steamboat on the Coosa River. The first such craft, named appropriately the USM (for United States Mail) *Coosa*, started running the river from Greensport, Alabama, to Rome and Calhoun in 1845. The small steamer had been built in Cincinnati and then run down the Ohio and Mississippi Rivers to the coast, on to Mobile and up the Alabama River to Wetumpka. There it was taken apart and loaded onto wagons in order to skirt a 138-mile series of rapids and shoals, to be put together again at Greensport. Piloted by Captain James Lafferty, the *Coosa* carried freight and mail between Rome and Alabama for many years.

The ever-present Colonel William Smith, soon thereafter, decided to get into the steamboat business in anticipation of a railroad line coming to Rome. Partnering with Major Hemphill, Smith commissioned the building of a hull by William Adkins. The boat was cristened the *William Smith* with great ceremony. When the railroad venture fell through, the *William Smith* mysteriously sank in the Oostanaula River, its hull visable for many years thereafter when the river ran low.

At least forty steamboats plied the waters of the Coosa and Oostanaula in the period between 1850 and 1900, carrying a great deal of cotton, lumber, farming supplies and other items. As early as 1847, the steamboats were carrying 12,000 bales of cotton to

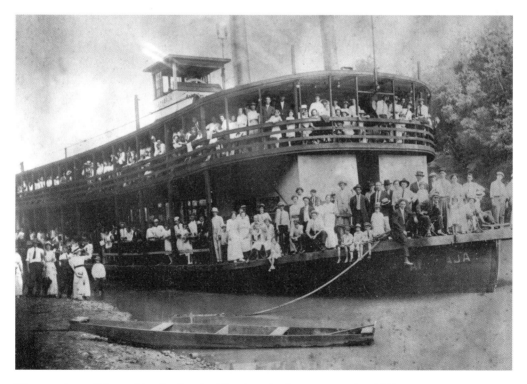

The steamboat *Alabama* with a few hundred Sunday school passengers, circa 1900.

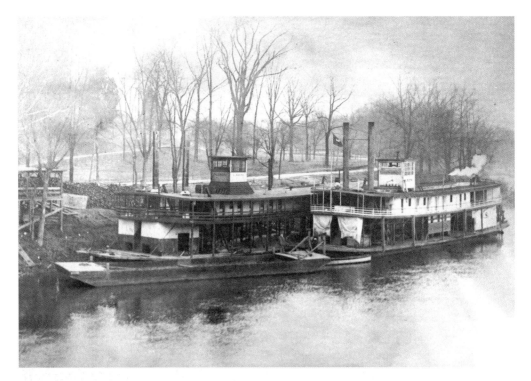

Two steamboats, the *Alabama* and the *Leota*, dock to load fuel before picking up passengers and freight.

Rome to be transferred to wagons and then on to the Western and Atlantic Railroad connection in Kingston. The inventory on the steamer *Undine*, arriving in Rome in the 1870s, listed as its cargo 357 bales of cotton, 40,0000 shingles, 625 pelts, 50 cowhides, 50 baskets of poultry, 200 bushels of corn, 250 bags of wheat and 27 passengers.

Among the steamboats of the period were the *Dixie*, the *John J. Seay*, the *Hill City*, the *Sidney P. Smith*, the *Alfarata*, the *Connasauga*, the *Calhoun* and the *Etowah Bill*. The *Magnolia*, at 160 feet in length and 36 feet wide, was the undisputed queen of the river. She kept a crew of twenty-five, not including the cooks, waiters and maids who maintained the impressive passenger lounge and staterooms. The *Magnolia* sunk near Centre, Alabama, in 1881, but the boat whistle was saved. In February of 1939, at the dedication of the H.H. Keel levee, the whistle was blown one last time during a parade by Wallace Grant from the top of the Rome Laundry Company on West Fourth Avenue.

FERRIES AND BRIDGES

Rivers have often been called the interstate highways of the eighteenth and nineteenth centuries, carrying goods and people to destinations across the country. In fact, it was almost impossible to establish a town without access to waterways before the coming of the railroad. The problem with rivers was that they often did not flow in the direction

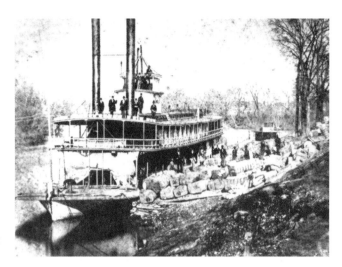

The steamboat *Magnolia* being loaded with baled cotton.

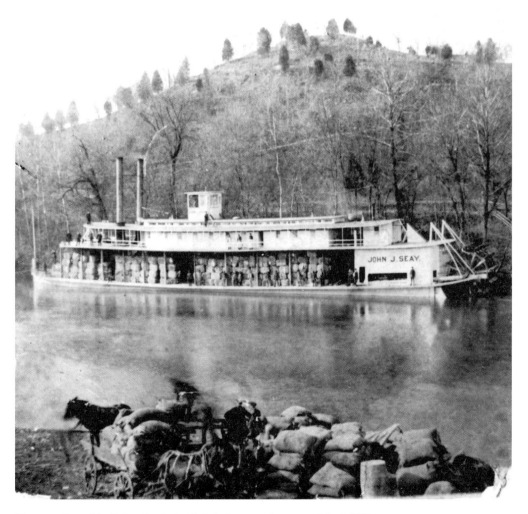

The steamboat *John J. Seay*, loaded with baled cotton, floats past Myrtle Hill.

that you wanted them to flow. Furthermore, sometimes you just wanted to cross them to get to the other side. This could be a dangerous proposition for man and beast. Shallow fords across rivers had to be found. These fords were often seasonal, gone during the spring floods and bone dry during the summer, so enterprising businessmen often built ferryboats and landings at strategic points on the rivers.

It is difficult to pin down the total number of ferries in Floyd County in the 1800s. The Ross Ferry, also known as the Forks Ferry, was located at the junction of the three rivers. It may have been there as early as the Battle of Etowah in 1793. Passengers could cross any of the three rivers using this ferryboat. Records show that Thomas H. Clyatt received the title to the lot upon which the ferry was located during the 1832 Land Lottery, dispossessing John Ross of much of his property. Eventually that important ferry crossing came under the control of Zachariah Hargrove and William Smith. An early court record from 1838 reported that Marshall Ligon of Coweta County paid seventy-five cents a wagon to cross on the ferry. It sank, causing a loss of property and the life of a Negro boy slave belonging to Ligon. He sued both Hargrove and Smith but died before the case came before the court.

Roger Aycock, in his book *All Roads to Rome*, reports that David Hutchins was authorized to establish a ferry across the Oostanaula on his land. He charged 50 cents for each four-horse wagon, 25 cents for an oxcart, 12½ cents for each man on horseback, 6¼ cents

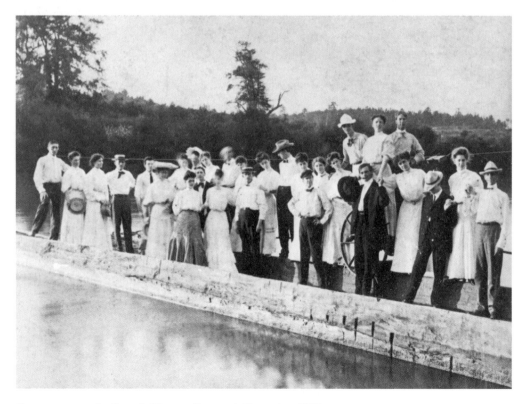

Passengers cross the Etowah River on Freeman's Ferry, circa 1900.

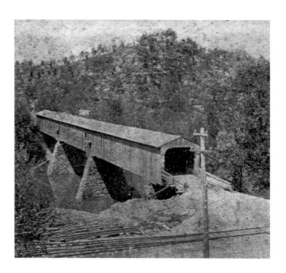

The original covered bridge over the Etowah River at the foot of Myrtle Hill.

for each single horse, 3 cents for each head of cattle and 2 cents for sheep, goats and hogs. This ferry eventually became known as Bell's Ferry and operated until 1954. Other ferries on the Oostanaula included Pope's Ferry, Johnson's Ferry and Miller's Ferry. On the Etowah River, Freeman's Ferry, Bass's Ferry and the Woodley Ferry crossed the river between Rome and Kingston. The coming of steamboats on the rivers caused problems for ferryboat operators who used cables. Eventually steamboat pilots blew a whistle to warn ferry operators of their approach, allowing them time to drop their cables in the water so the boats could pass over them.

It is not possible to set an exact date for the building of the first two bridges in Rome. A company headed by Afred Shorter, Dr. H.V.M. Miller and Lewis Tumlin apparently built two bridges in the period between 1840 and 1851: one over the Etowah River at the foot of Broad Street and another over the Oostanaula River at West Second Avenue. In 1851, William R. Smith, known as "Long Will" due to his long hair (not related to the founder of the same name), received authorization to build a bridge over the Oostanaula River at West Fifth Avenue. Shorter and his company sued but were rejected by the court.

Eventually Long Will was unable to come up with the money to build the bridge and the contract reverted to Shorter's company. In an agreement with the city, Shorter agreed to demolish the Second Avenue Bridge and build a better covered bridge at Fifth Avenue with reduced tolls. The Fifth Avenue bridge cost $15,000 to build. Both the Etowah and Oostanaula bridges are shown in Ballou's newspaper illustration of 1856. They were destroyed by the Union army in 1864.

THE COMING OF THE RAILROAD

In 1836, the state of Georgia established a state-owned railroad known as the Western and Atlantic (W&A) to open Georgia to the trade of the Tennessee and Ohio Rivers.

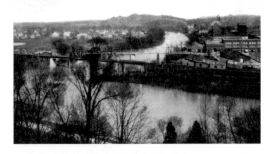

Left: postcard view of the railroad bridge across the Oostanaula River; the Etowah River flows in the foreground.

Below: A train crosses South Broad Street as a railroad employee alerts traffic.

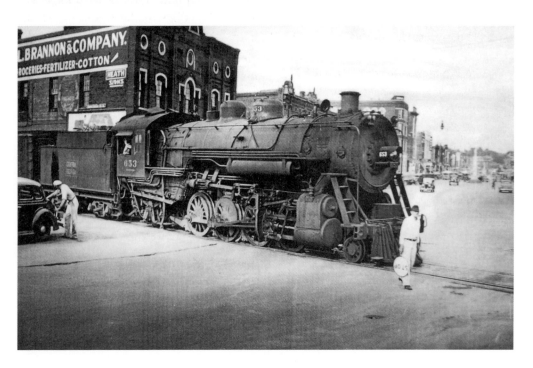

Beginning at Terminus (Atlanta), the railroad would run to Chattanooga. Several route proposals were submitted, including one from Colonel William Smith to include Rome along the route and to even make Rome the destination or northern terminus of the line. The powerful interests in Chattanooga, led by James Whiteside, did everything in their power to kill the Rome as terminus proposal, going so far as to attempt to bribe Colonel Smith with a new mansion in Chattanooga.

Eventually the Chattanooga forces won out. The line came all the way to Kingston, sixteen miles from Rome, before turning north to the Tennessee border through Dalton. However, the founding fathers of the town would not long be denied. The Memphis Branch Railroad and Steamboat Company received a charter in 1839 with the goal of connecting the Coosa River at Rome with the new state railroad. It changed its name to the Rome Railroad Company in January 1850, soon after completing a twenty-mile rail line from Rome to the W&A at Kingston.

Another railroad, chartered originally in 1848 as the Alabama and Tennessee River Railroad, became the Selma, Rome and Dalton Railroad. Construction of this route was interrupted by the Civil War, but the road eventually reached Dalton in 1870. It was reorganized as the Georgia Southern Railroad in 1874. A rail line from Rome to Macon was completed in 1882. The Rome and Decatur Line was organized in 1886. Finally, most of these lines merged to form the Southern Railway Company in 1895. Other shorter lines were built between Rome and Coosa and Rome and Carrolton as part of the Chattanooga, Rome and Columbus Railroad.

Goods from throughout the Coosa River Valley could now travel by steamboat to a railhead at Rome to reach the rest of the world. The editor of the *Courier* practically beamed in an article entitled "Rome, Its Prospects," published in February of 1851:

> *It is gratifying to watch the gradual but certain growth of our young and vigorous city…Since the completion of the "Rome Railroad," business has steadily increased, and under a wise and liberal policy will be largely augmented during the next few years. If we are not greatly deceived, Rome will double its population of more than 3,000 in the next four years…Its population with the exception of some 20 to 30 very clever doctors and lawyers, (who, we are happy to say, have but little to do), is made up mostly of substantial business men who are permanently identified with the place and deeply interested in its prosperity and reputation. Surrounded by a country of unsurpassed beauty and fertility, occupied by an unusually dense and valuable agricultural population—at the terminus of railroad and steamboat transportation—Rome is and must ever continue to be a place of considerable commercial importance.*

CHAPTER THREE

THE LATE, GREAT UNPLEASANTNESS

FLOYD COUNTY AND ROME IN 1860

By 1860, Georgia's population had reached over 1 million. Of that total, 44 percent were slaves, although only 41,000 of the 595,000 free citizens of the state were slaveholders. The four largest cities in the state were Savannah (22,000), Augusta (12,000), Columbus (9,600) and Atlanta (9,500). Floyd County showed a population of 15,233, with 35 percent (5,297) of its inhabitants being held in bondage. The total value of the slaves in the county was $3,755,184, only slightly less than the total value of all the rest of the property—$3,885,951. The average value of each slave was $651.70, while the average value of each acre of land was $9.30. The county's population had almost doubled in the preceding ten years. Rome, with a population slightly over 4,000, was twice as big as Chattanooga, Tennessee. It was well on its way to becoming one of the most prosperous cities in Georgia. And then the war came.

Whatever its name—the War of Yankee Aggression, the War for Constitutional Liberty, the War for Southern Independence, the Second American Revolution, the War for States' Rights, Mr. Lincoln's War, the War of the Southern Planters, the War of the Rebellion, the War to Suppress Yankee Arrogance, the Brothers' War, the War Against Slavery, the Lost Cause, the War Between the States—the American Civil War was the seminal event in our history. Between 1861 and 1865, over 650,000 Americans would die in the first modern war of the age. Billions of dollars worth of property would be destroyed and hundreds of thousands of people would be left homeless. Rome and Floyd County would not be spared the horrors of this war. The consequences of the conflict continue to echo to this day.

SECESSION

In northwest Georgia, many citizens maintained strong Union sentiments. However, the social (slavery), political (states' rights) and economic (tariffs, taxes, growth of industry in the North) issues of the day, coupled with the election of Abraham Lincoln on November 6, 1860, led many in the South to believe that the time was ripe to leave the

Union. Six days after Lincoln's election and thirty-nine days prior to the secession of South Carolina (the first state to do so on December 20, 1860), the citizens of Rome held a large mass meeting to discuss the crisis and pass a series of resolutions. The editor of the *Rome Southerner* newspaper reported, "We never saw resolutions pass more unanimously or more enthusiastically. To some of the resolutions there was one or two dissenting voices. Most of them, however, passed unanimously. We were sorry to see even a single person in that large assembly who withheld his assent." The following is included in A.D. Candler's *The Confederate Records of the State of Georgia*:

> *Resolutions on Secession from Floyd County, Georgia, November 12, 1860*
> *Floyd County is where Rome, Georgia, is located.*
> *Whereas the abolition sentiment of the Northern States first openly manifested in 1820, has for the last forty years, steadily and rapidly increased in volume, and in the intensity of hostility to the form of society, existing in the Southern States, and to the rights of these States as equal, independent, and sovereign members of the Union; has led to long continued and ever increasing abuse and hatred of the Southern people; to ceaseless war upon their plainest Constitutional rights; to an open and shameless nullification of that provision of the constitution intended to secure the rendition of fugitive slaves, and of the laws of Congress to give it effect…has prompted the armed invasion of Southern soil, by stealth…for the diabolical purpose of inaugurating a ruthless war of the blacks against the whites throughout the Southern States; has prompted large masses of Northern people openly to sympathize with the treacherous and traitorous invaders of our country, and elevate the leader of a band of midnight assassins, and robbers…to the rank of a hero and a martyr…has disrupted the churches and destroyed all national parties, and has now finally organized a party confined to a hostile section, and composed even there of those only who have encouraged, sympathized with, instigated, or perpetuated their long series of insults, outrages, and wrongs, for the avowed purpose of making a common government, armed by us with power only for our protection, an instrument, in the hands of enemies for our destruction.*
>
> *Therefore, we, the people of Floyd County…do hereby declare:*
> *1st. That Georgia is and of right ought to be a free, sovereign and independent state.*
> *2d. That she came into the Union with the other states, as a sovereignty, and by virtue of that sovereignty, has the right to secede whenever, in her sovereign capacity, she shall judge such a step necessary.*
> *3d. That in our opinion, she ought not to submit to the inauguration of Abraham Lincoln and Hannibal Hamlin, as her President and Vice-President; but should leave them to rule over those by whom alone they were elected.*
> *4th. That we request the Legislature to announce this opinion…and to cooperate with the Governor in calling a Convention of the people to determine on the mode and measure of redress…*
> *5th. That we respectfully recommend to the Legislature to take into immediate consideration the passage of such laws as will be likely to alleviate any unusual embarrassment of the commercial interests of the State…*

6th. That we respectfully suggest to the Legislature to take immediate steps to organize and arm the forces of the State…

7th. That copies of the foregoing resolutions be sent without delay to our Senators and Representatives in the General Assembly of the State.

When words and phrases like "increasing abuse and hatred," "diabolical purpose," "ruthless war," "treacherous and traitorous invaders," "midnight assassins and robbers," "long series of insults" and "outrages and wrongs" are used in public resolutions, it is easy to gauge the passions that dominated the times. On December 3, 1860, in a meeting of Floyd County residents at city hall, cooler heads prevailed "in an earnest effort to maintain [Georgia's] rights, secure her liberties and vindicate her honor." Resolutions were sent demanding Northern concessions in repealing personal liberty laws, in the return of fugitive slaves and "the right of Southern citizens to settle with their negro property in any territory of the United States."

On January 16, 1861, following the secession from the Union of South Carolina, Alabama and Florida, delegates from Georgia met in the state capitol at Milledgeville to consider withdrawal from the United States. By a closer than expected vote of 166 to 130, a majority voted for secession. The three Floyd County delegates—Colonel James Word, Colonel Simpson Fouche and Francis C. Shropshire—all voted for secession, as did 35 of the 49 delegates from northwest Georgia. As a symbol of the terrible division in families that the war would cause, Wesley Shropshire, a delegate from Chattooga County, the father of Francis, voted against his son in favor of remaining in the Union (his son would die for the cause in Kentucky in 1862). Three months later, the firing of the first shots at Fort Sumter in Charleston, South Carolina, signaled the beginning of the conflict.

GONE FOR A SOLDIER

Rome soon became a central point for militia troops to gather in the northwestern part of the state. With eyes bright and easy victory assured, Rome and Floyd County volunteers formed companies, elected officers, got rudimentary training and were transported to Northern Virginia and other battle fronts. Along with the Rome Light Guards, the Floyd Infantry, the Floyd Sharpshooters and other local companies, the Miller Rifles, under Captain John R. Towers, saw heavy action in the first major battle of the war at Manassas, Virginia. The ninety-eight men of the Miller Rifles left Rome on May 29, 1861. The *Rome Weekly Courier* reported that the company was made up of "the best kind of fighting men." Three members of the Rome Light Guards married their hometown sweethearts before their departure to the war front in Virginia in 1861. Prominent among them was Captain E.J. Magruder, recently graduated from Virginia Military Institute, who married Miss Florence Fouche. The dashing young captain eventually was wounded six times during the war but returned to Rome. He and his wife are buried at Myrtle Hill Cemetery.

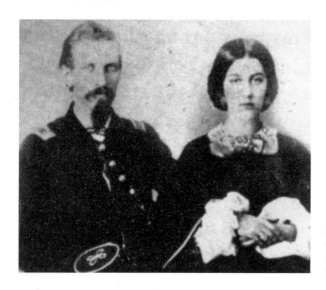

Captain Edwin Jones Magruder and his wife, Florence Fouche Magruder, were married prior to his going off to fight in the Civil War.

In all, twenty units from Floyd County, comprising approximately two thousand men, including Home Guards, volunteered or were drafted into the service of the Confederacy. Most did not return. Of the 110 members of the Floyd Sharpshooters who went to war in 1861, for example, only 10 were still around to surrender at Appomattox Court House in 1865.

BILL ARP

Before Mark Twain there was Bill Arp. Charles Henry Smith, born in Lawrenceville, Georgia, in 1826, studied law, started a large family and moved to Rome in 1851. The story goes that one day soon after Abraham Lincoln's proclamation calling for seventy-five thousand troops to put down the Southern rebellion following Fort Sumter, Smith was sitting on the courthouse steps writing a satirical reply. A local cracker named Bill Arp, who could neither read nor write, heard the letter and asked that his name be signed to the brazen epistle. The legend of Bill Arp was born.

Rome, Ga. Aprile, 1861
Mr. Linkhorn, Sur:
We have received your proklamation, and as you have put us on very short notis, a few of us boys have konkluded to write to you, and ask for a little more time…It is utterly unpossible for us to disperse in thirty days; I tried my darndest yesterday to disperse and retire, but it was no go…Most of the boys here are so hot they fairly siz, when you pour water on 'em, and that's the way they make up their military companies here now—when a man applies to jine the volunteers, they sprinkle him, and if he sizzes, they take him, and if he don't, they don't…Your proklamations says something about taking possession of private property "at all Hazards," but we can't find no such place on the map…One

man said it was a little faktory on an iland in Lake Champlain where they made sand
bags. My opinion is that the sand business won't pay, and is a great waste of money. Our
boys here carry there sand in their gizzards, where is keeps better, and is always handy.

The letter to "Mr. Linkhorn, Sur" made Bill Arp a household name as it was reprinted across the South. Smith wrote almost thirty more Arp letters for Southern newspapers during the war. Most attacked Union policies and praised the Confederacy even in the desperate times of 1864 and 1865. His description of his family's experiences as refugees ("runagees," he called them) from his East Fourth Avenue home in Rome while fleeing from Sherman's Federal troops in 1864 is humorous and good-natured. Later, after the war, Smith often expressed a good bit of frustration, even anger, when discussing the Reconstruction policies of the country. He served as mayor of Rome in 1867–68 and completed one term in the state legislature before becoming disgusted in general with "pollytix." The Arp letters ended, for a time, in the early 1870s. Smith moved to Cartersville, Georgia, in 1877 and soon began a twenty-five-year series of Arp letters for the *Atlanta Constitution*. He died in 1903 and is buried in the Oak Hill Cemetery in Cartersville.

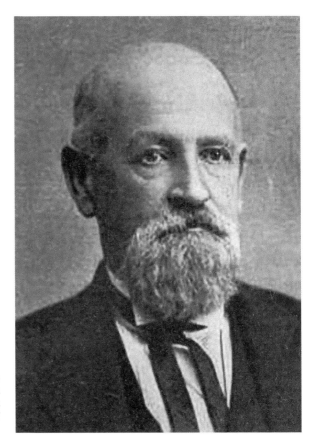

"What is to be, will be, whether it happens or not." Charles H. "Bill Arp" Smith, a citizen of Rome for twenty-six years, was one of the great Southern humorists of the nineteenth century.

NOBLE FOUNDRY

Ironically, a few kind words of promotion and the courtesy of two Roman businessmen led to Rome becoming a target of the Federal army during the Civil War. In 1855, James R. Noble Sr. and his six sons, noted iron makers from England by way of Pennsylvania, were looking for new opportunities in the South. They had decided to settle in Chattanooga, but upon a chance meeting with Rome businessman John Hume Sr. and banker Wade S. Cothran, they changed their minds. Ever the Southern gentlemen, Hume and Cothran convinced the elder Noble that Rome's potential for growth was greater than that of the city on the Tennessee River (thus beginning the long tradition of Rome's ability to charm outside industry into the region, which continues to this day).

As it was, the move to Rome almost did not happen. On a train from Charleston, South Carolina, James Noble Sr. had a carpetbag with $3,000 to $4,000 stolen from his baggage car. Two strangers who had boarded the train at a later stop and had traveled in the same car were soon arrested by an officer summoned by the elder Noble. The two politely, but with feeling, proclaimed their innocence, the taller and thinner of the two explaining that he was Jefferson Davis, secretary of war under the administration of President Franklin Pierce. The money was never recovered, although many years later a Catholic priest informed the family by letter that the conductor of the train had confessed on his deathbed to the crime.

Without money, the Nobles depended on the credit extended by banker Cothran, but soon had their foundry up and running on the banks of the Etowah River near the lower end of Broad Street. An immense lathe (sixteen feet long) used by the brothers was transported by ship to Mobile, Alabama, from Nashua, New Hampshire. After a journey up the Alabama and Coosa Rivers, falls west of Rome forced the company to unpack and dismantle the lathe, which they finished transporting by ox cart.

Soon after the war started, the Noble Brothers Foundry began making three-inch rifled cannons, twelve-pound smoothbore howitzers, siege guns and bronze six- and

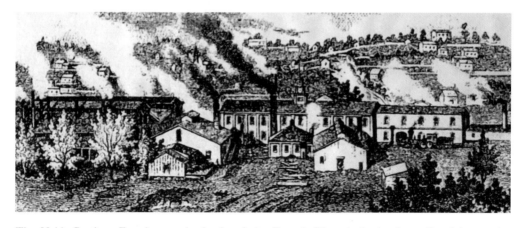

The Noble Brothers Foundry, on the banks of the Etowah River, built the first railroad locomotive manufactured south of Richmond, Virginia. It became a target of Yankee raiders during the Civil War.

twelve-pound smoothbore cannons, along with caissons, carriages and limbers for the Confederacy. By presidential order, Jefferson Davis, who had become friends with the Nobles after the embarrassing train incident, declared that no Noble family son could enlist or be drafted into the Confederate army. "We have plenty of men who can fight," he declared, "but few who can make cannon."

When General Sherman's army captured and then left Rome in 1864, the buildings of the Noble Foundry were destroyed. However, the lathe, although severely damaged, was not. It continued in service until 1972, when it was purchased by the Rome Area Heritage Foundation and placed under a shelter at the city's Civic Center. The Noble family rebuilt the plant after the Civil War and began manufacturing railroad cars, eventually transferring the business to Anniston, Alabama. Until recent times, cannonballs test fired by the Nobles were occasionally found across the Etowah River from the site of the foundry, buried on the eastern slope of Mount Aventine or in the riverbank below.

A HOSPITAL TOWN

With its location on the Coosa River, the railroad spur connection to the Western and Atlantic Railroad and the fact that the city was still a comfortable distance from the front lines of the war, Rome became a logical place for wounded soldiers to convalesce. In November of 1862, Confederate military authorities toured the city to see if there were enough available shelters and resources to support army hospitals. In August of 1862, a Soldiers' Relief Room, founded by the Soldier's Aid Society, had been established on the corner of Broad Street and East First Avenue, but it was not designed or equipped to be a hospital. Unfortunately, in early November of 1862, one of the soldiers (William Lynch of the Ninth Louisiana Regiment, age seventeen) recently arrived was found to have smallpox. The panic caused by the news of the arrival of this dreaded disease in Rome can only be imagined. The Rome *Courier* cautioned its readers to keep off the streets and get vaccinated: "Let everyone keep cool, and do not be alarmed, as fear is a powerful agent in the spread of the disease." Eventually Private Lynch recovered and the building was burned to the ground.

By December of 1862, a Confederate Military Hospital had been established along the 400 block of Broad Street (the Lumpkin Hospital), causing several local businesses to relocate in the city. The Quintard Hospital at Broad Street and Fifth Avenue and the Bell Hospital located in the old Oddfellows Hall soon followed. The establishment of these hospitals could not have happened soon enough. On December 31, 1862, and January 2, 1863, the bloody Battle of Stones River was fought in Murfreesboro, Tennessee (the opposing armies had taken New Year's Day off before continuing to kill each other). Soon over 1,100 wounded and dying Confederate soldiers were crowded into Rome's hospitals. The strain of a 25 percent increase in the city's population soon became evident. The commissary department sent out a request for 50,000 pounds of soap, 3,000 yards of homespun cloth, 1,000 pounds of beef per day, chickens, flour, eggs, butter, vegetables, etc., which stripped the countryside and created shortages that became greater as the war progressed.

In March of 1863, a fourth hospital was established on the west side of the 200 block specifically for the officers of General Leonidas Polk's Army Corps. The recovering inmates of the Polk Hospital soon added much to social gatherings in the city during the summer of 1863. As the war zones inched closer to Rome, the Quintard Hospital staff and some equipment moved to Cleveland, Tennessee, but the building quickly became the site of the Pim Hospital.

Many of the finest doctors and surgeons in the South served in Rome's hospitals during the war. Dr. Homer Virgil Milton Miller of Rome, known as the "Demosthenes of the Mountains" for his political oratory, took charge of the Bell Hospital. Dr. L.T. Pim served as chief surgeon, while Dr. R.W. Hall directed operations at the smallpox vaccination center. Kate Cumming, who often is called the "Clara Barton of the South," served as a nurse in Rome during the summer of 1863. She noted in her diary, "I was very much pleased with the appearance of Rome. Like the renowned city, the name of which it bears, it is built on several hills. It has some very handsome buildings; the principal streets are broad and clean. There are many handsome store buildings, and they were pretty well supplied with goods, and cheaper than I have seen any place in the Confederacy."

The finest physician in Rome's first thirty years was Dr. Robert Battey. He was born near Augusta, Georgia, in 1828. His parents, Cephas and Mary Magruder Battey, died while he was a small child. He and a brother, George Battey (the only two of five children who lived to maturity), became wards of their uncle, Dr. George Magruder, who lived in Columbia County, Georgia. He attended school at Augusta, Georgia, and at Phillips Academy in Andover, Massachusetts. In January of 1848, he went into the drug business at Rome, Georgia, with a Dr. Dickerson. His business prospered and on December 20, 1849, he married Miss Martha B. Smith of Rome. For several years, beginning in 1853 or earlier, he studied pharmacy, chemistry and medicine in Philadelphia. He graduated from Jefferson Medical College in 1857 and began practice in Rome, Georgia.

In September 1859, he attended a medical association meeting in Boston and from there he went to England, Ireland, Scotland and then to Paris, where he studied medicine for several months. He was cordially received by surgeons wherever he went. They were particularly interested in Battey's Operation, a technique he developed concerned with removal of the ovaries. He later became known for this operation. Mrs. Battey frequently assisted Dr. Battey with his operations. He eventually established the Martha Battey Hospital at Rome, Georgia, in her honor.

During the Civil War, Dr. Battey served as a surgeon in the Confederate army. He began as senior surgeon of Hampton's brigade in July 1861 and later served in hospitals in Atlanta, Rome and Vineville, Georgia, and Lauderdale, Mississippi. His last assignment (until May 1865) was in Macon, Georgia, where he was in charge of a hospital. In 1873, he became professor of obstetrics at the Atlanta Medical College, where he remained until 1875. Dr. Battey continued the practice of medicine until his death in 1895. A monument to his service stands on the lawn of Rome's City Auditorium.

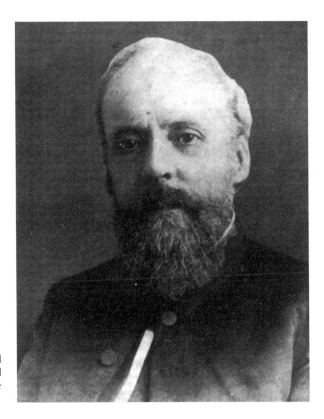

Dr. Robert Battey was considered Rome's greatest surgeon. He was placed in temporary charge of Confederate hospitals in Rome during the Civil War.

A RAID AND A RIDE

Things were not going well for the Confederacy in the spring of 1863. Although General Lee's Army of Northern Virginia had once again beaten back another Union invasion at the Battle of Chancellorsville in May, he had lost his best general, Thomas "Stonewall" Jackson, shot by his own men by mistake while advancing on the field. In the west, General Ulysses S. Grant had finally found a way to approach Vicksburg and lay siege to the last Confederate city on the Mississippi River. To keep the pressure on the South, and in advance of Union General Rosecrans's move to Chattanooga, several cavalry raids deep into the heartland of the Confederacy were attempted.

In late April, 1863, Union Colonel Abel D. Streight was given the mission to destroy the towns, bridges, foundries, railroads and commissary supplies along a route from central Tennessee through Gadsden, Alabama, Rome and Dalton. One of his prime objectives was to destroy the Noble Foundry in Rome. His command of two thousand men, unfortunately mounted on generally unbroken and stubborn mules, was made up of the Fifty-first and Seventy-third Indiana, Eightieth Illinois and Third Ohio Cavalry units.

Upon news of Streight's Raid, the famous Confederate cavalryman General Nathan B. Forrest, with five hundred mounted Confederate troops, began pursuit. Although the Union forces had an eighty-mile head start, Forrest's men soon caught up with Streight's brigade, thus beginning a series of running battles to the Georgia border. Along the way, Forrest received help from a young sixteen-year-old girl named Emma Sansom, who personally, under fire, directed Forrest to a ford on the Black River in Alabama. Having burned the bridge on the Black River, Streight's command moved to Gadsden, Alabama, staying only long enough to destroy a supply of flour, five hundred stands of arms and the ferryboat before heading to Georgia. Streight then sent two hundred men of his command under Captain Milton Russell on to Rome with orders to capture the city and hold the bridges until the arrival of the main force.

Forty-two-year-old John H. Wisdom lived in Gadsden, Alabama. He was exempt from army service because of his duties as a ferryboat operator and mail carrier. On May 2, 1863, he found that Union soldiers had cut a hole in his ferryboat and learned that they were on their way to Rome. He decided to ride to Rome, sixty-seven miles away, to warn the citizens that the Yankees were coming. He was originally from Rome and a significant factor in his decision to make the ride was that his mother still lived there. At about 3:30 p.m., he hitched his horse to his two-wheeling buggy and began his eight-and-a-half-hour journey.

Five horses, one mule and one bad fall later, Wisdom crossed the wooden bridge over the Etowah into Rome at midnight. The owner of the Etowah Hotel asked him to ride up and down the streets to warn the people of the impending raid. That being done, his work was finished and he "went to the home of his mother, who lived in Rome, and went to bed."

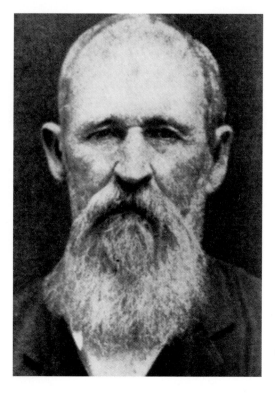

John Wisdom, the "Paul Revere of the South," rode sixty-seven miles from Gadsden, Alabama, to warn Romans of Streight's Raid.

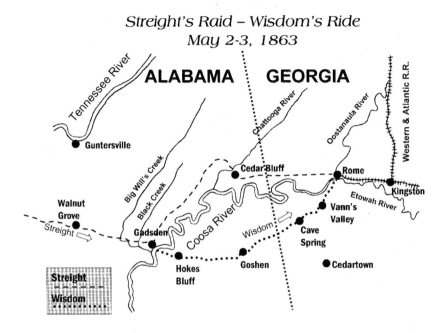

Streight's raid and Wisdom's ride, May 2–3, 1863. *Map by the author.*

Within thirty minutes, Wisdom was probably the only man in town who was asleep. Breastworks were hastily put up along the outer roads of the city, turpentine and straw were laid along the bridge with the intent to burn the crossing and several hundred old men and boys with squirrel guns and shotguns prepared to meet the Yankee invaders. Captain Russell's advance guard of two hundred Union cavalrymen arrived outside the city around noon on May 3, 1863. Questioning an elderly black woman, he was told that thousands of Confederate soldiers were stationed in Rome. Scanning the breastworks in front of him, he decided to wait for the main body before attempting to take the city, thus saving the lives of the unorganized militia and the city from the torch.

Finally, on May 3, 1863, exhausted by daily battles and night long rides, Streight's men were overtaken by the Confederate troops near Cedar Bluff, Alabama. General Forrest then played a card that he used many times during the war. During a parlay with Colonel Streight, he had his men march several times around a clearing and moved his only cannon to different locations in an attempt to convince Streight that he was outnumbered, a fact that was not true. Streight fell for the bluff and surrendered his 1,566 men. He protested vigorously after finding out about the deception, but he and his men were taken to Rome as prisoners. General Forrest was fêted in Rome, given a beautiful horse named Highlander (who later was killed at the Battle of Chickamauga) by the citizens of the city and soon moved on to other theaters of the war.

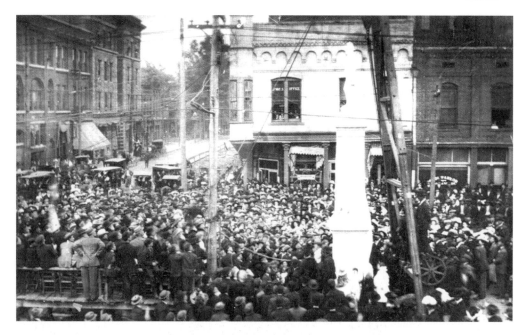

A monument to Confederate General Nathan Bedford Forrest was dedicated on Broad Street in 1909. Eventually becoming an impediment to traffic, it was moved to Myrtle Hill Cemetery.

The news of Streight's surrender to General Forrest soon changed the scene in Rome from one of terror to pure joy. For his actions, the grateful citizens gave John Wisdom a silver tea service worth $400 and $300 in cash. Each year, the John Wisdom Wagon Train and Trail Ride is held along the route taken by the "Paul Revere of the South." Several pieces of Wisdom's tea service are now on exhibit at the Rome Area History Museum.

"THE STRONGEST FORTIFIED PLACE IN DIXIE"

After Streight's abortive raid in 1863, the citizens of Rome and Floyd County quickly organized to defend their community. Among the measures adopted was the expenditure of $3,000 to construct fortifications on the hills around Rome. Between July 13 and October 9, 1863, military engineer Captain James F. Laulor was in charge of the construction of these forts, using the labor of slaves from local farms, hired for the project (slave owners were paid $2 per slave per day).

In September, three of these forts were named for local Confederate soldiers who had died in the war: Fort Attaway, on the west bank of the Oostanaula River; Fort Stoval, on the south bank of the Etowah River; and Fort Norton, north of the city on the east bank of the Oostanaula. By Christmas of 1863, work on these forts was taken over by the army of Tennessee. Soldiers "convicted of various crimes by a recent court martial" were sent to the city to work "at hard labor upon the fortifications around this town."

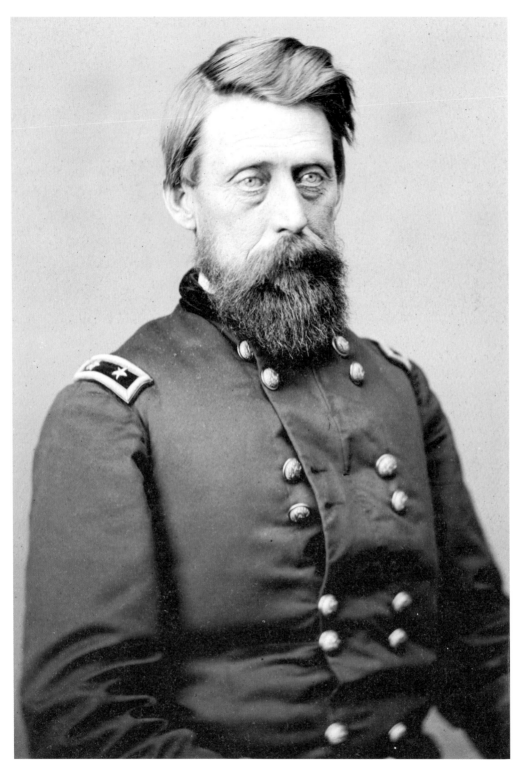

General Jefferson C. Davis commanded the Federal troops that first entered Rome on May 18, 1864. *Courtesy of the Library of Congress.*

Union spies sent by General Grenville Dodge took note of the string of fortifications and trenches being built in Rome. Alarmed at threatening moves by Sherman's army, General Joseph Johnston sent a telegram to Rome on April 24, 1864. "Complete the defenses as soon as quickly as possible. Use the labor of troops. Let the engineers get Negroes also if practical." After nearly a year in construction, the defenses of Rome were apparently very strong.

Following the Battle of Resaca in mid-May 1864, Union General William T. Sherman sent a portion of his army, under the command of General Jefferson C. Davis (no relation to the Confederate president), to capture the city of Rome. As he approached the city on May 17, Davis halted and sent back a report to Sherman: "The works [of the city] looked so strong, I thought it imprudent to storm them hastily." But the five thousand Confederate troops at Rome were under orders to pull out. Texas troops were ordered to sack the town of any portable supplies, removing $150,000 worth of provisions and clothing before beating a hasty retreat. The bridge over the Oostanaula River was burned. Quickly building a pontoon bridge nearby, Davis's division soon captured the city. Members of the Eighty-fifth Illinois had the honor of being the first "Yankee" troops in Rome. Proud of this feat, Davis reported to headquarters on May 18 that his Northern troops were "in possession of the strongest fortified place I have seen in Dixie."

General Johnston's decision to withdraw troops from Rome and retreat from strong positions in Cassville has often been criticized. With hindsight, had he held Rome's forts with the five thousand men stationed there, he could have diverted a whole division of the Union army while inflicting much harm on the rest of Sherman's divided force. General Sherman had called the Etowah River the "Rubicon of the South." Once he gained a foothold across the Etowah at Rome, he considered the fall of Atlanta to be a foregone conclusion. A defeat at the Etowah would have stalled his offensive and perhaps delayed the fall of Atlanta past the presidential elections in November of 1864. The defeat of Abraham Lincoln at the polls that year may have resulted in the independence of the Southern states. The fall of Rome led to the fall of the Confederacy.

SHERMAN

For the next six months, the city of Rome was occupied by Federal troops. Reuben S. Norton, the keeper of the city's first weather information, estimated in his diary that twenty-five thousand Union troops could be found in the area around Rome. The churches in town were soon put into service. The pews of the Presbyterian church were used to make a pontoon bridge; the church itself became a storehouse for hard bread. The Methodist church became an ammunition dump, while other churches became stables for Federal army horses. Much of the citizenry of the city had moved to the countryside. Rome had become an armed camp.

After the fall of Atlanta in September of 1864, the Rebel army, now under the command of General John B. Hood, moved north, hoping to strike a fatal blow to

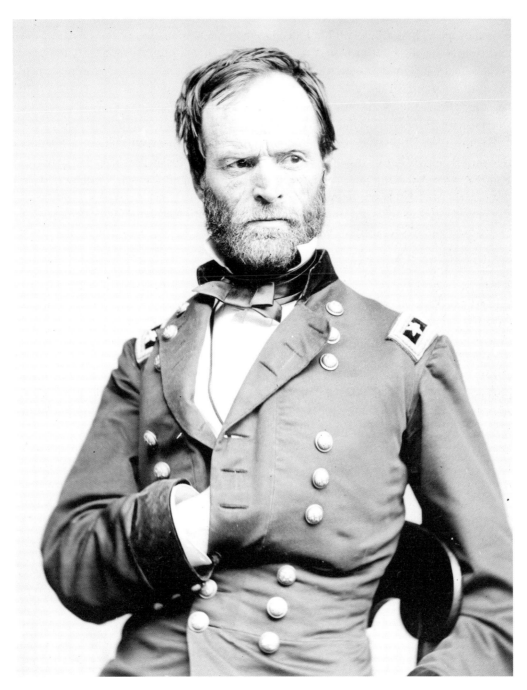

General William Tecumseh Sherman had his headquarters in Rome for several weeks in 1864. He received permission to proceed with his March to the Sea while in the city. *Courtesy of the Library of Congress.*

Sherman's communications. This movement threatened Rome, so the city's defenses were rebuilt by Union forces. On October 28, 1864, General Sherman himself entered the city in pursuit but soon decided to allow Hood to escape to the north, knowing that other Federal troops could handle the impetuous Confederate commander. Here Sherman received the telegram from General U.S. Grant approving his plan to "March to the Sea." Rome had lost its strategic value and its days were numbered.

Not wishing to leave anything of military value behind, Sherman ordered the destruction of the city. A copy of General Sherman's order of November 10, 1864, to Brigadier-General John Corse, commander of Union forces in Rome, reads:

> *In the execution of sealed orders No. 115, you will destroy tonight all public property not needed by your command, all foundries, mills, workshops, warehouses, railroad depots, all other storehouses convenient to the railroad, together with the wagonshops, tanneries, or other factories useful to our enemy. Destroy the bridges completely, and then move tomorrow to Kingston or beyond.*

Rome lay prostrate, crushed by this final blow. Reuben Norton noted that the destruction began about five o'clock that evening with the burning of the jail. By the morning of November 12, 1864, the Federal army had completely evacuated the city. After nearly four years of privation and six months of occupation by hostile troops, over two-thirds of the city was burned to the ground. Only forty citizens of a prewar population of nearly four thousand remained to defend the city from marauders and robbers. The war for Rome and Floyd County was over.

CHAPTER FOUR

FROM THE ASHES

THE DARK YEARS

Those citizens who remained in the city following its burning by Federal troops in November of 1864 must have felt a kinship to ancient Romans following the sacking of their city by the Vandals in AD 455. It is safe to say that the winter of 1864–65 was the darkest period in Rome's history. Almost everything of value had been destroyed or taken away by Sherman's men. Without the protection of Federal troops, however, Rome entered a period of lawlessness. Marauding bands of "independent scouts" occasionally entered the city to steal the leftovers. Several elderly citizens of the town were injured or killed while attempting to protect their own property or the property of absent neighbors. Somehow they managed to get through the hard winter. As news of General Lee's surrender at Appomattox Court House on April 9, 1865, and General Johnston's surrender in North Carolina a few weeks later reached northern Georgia, those residents of the city who had fled started to return. With more men to patrol the streets as a volunteer guard, the danger of bandit raids subsided. Romans then turned to the task of cleaning away the rubble and rebuilding their city.

By the late summer of 1865, things were started to look a little better to the beleaguered citizens of Rome. Melville Dwinell, a former "Yankee" from Vermont, had moved to Rome in 1853 to become the editor of the *Courier*, a four-page weekly newspaper. On Thursday, August 31, 1865, after a fifteen-month absence, he renewed publication, renumbering the paper "Volume 20, New Series, No. 1." In this first edition he wrote,

To Former Patrons:
It would do no good to think hard things and still less to say wicked words; we at once resolved that as for us and our house, we would arise and go back to the old fold again. Well, the first thing to be done was to take the Amnesty Oath. Now about that we felt a little like the keeper of a cheap boarding house did about eating crow, after he had forced down a little for a wager. He said he could eat crow, but he "didn't hanker arter it!" We took the oath and have been feeling better ever since. It was probably just the medicine needed. We would advise every citizen of the state to embrace the first opportunity to take

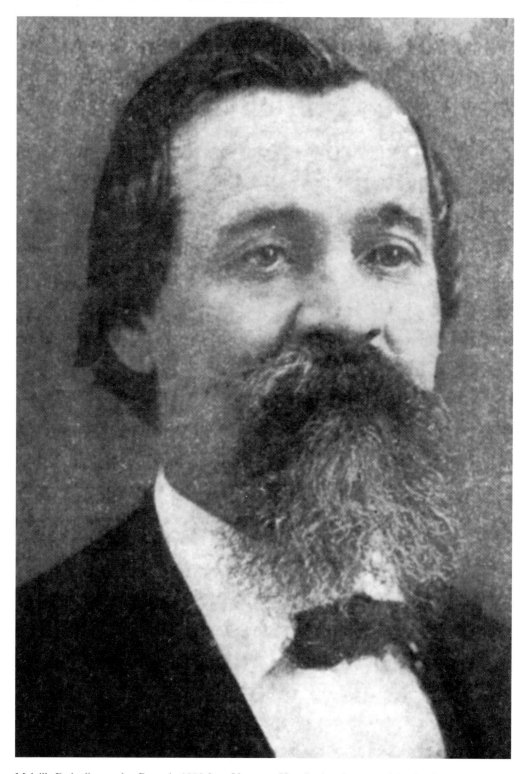

Melville Dwinell moved to Rome in 1853 from Vermont. He edited and managed the *Courier* for many years while remaining a committed bachelor for his entire life.

the Oath of Allegiance. It is as little as could possibly be asked of us after four years of most determined and earnest effort to disrupt the Federal Nation, and besides it is really our duty to give an honest pledge that hereafter we will give a full and cordial support of that government which after all our sins against it proposes now not only to pardon (with a few exceptions) but also to spread over us the aegis of its protecting wings.

It is not surprising to learn that many of Dwinell's patrons did not share his benevolent attitude, although on the same page he relates that 1,112 citizens of the city had already taken the Oath of Allegiance. He also reported in that same edition that both H.M. Anderson and the Noble brothers were preparing to rebuild their foundries. In addition, the businesses in Rome had increased to include twelve dry goods stores, nine groceries, two hotels, three saloons, two billiard rooms and two livery stables. Things were looking up.

Meanwhile, the political situation in Georgia approached chaos. Arguably suffering more than any other state in the Confederacy, Georgia had experienced the loss of forty thousand of its male citizens and millions of dollars in property damage. In June of 1865, President Andrew Johnson appointed a provisional governor, James Johnson of Columbus. A constitutional convention met in late October in Milledgeville to frame a new document that abolished slavery and repudiated the Confederate debt, hoping these measures would be enough to allow the state to reenter the Union. However, when new elections for state and federal officials were held in November of 1865, a vast majority of those elected were ex-Confederate leaders, including Alexander Stevens, former vice president of the Confederacy.

Northern politicians were outraged by this flagrant example of defiance; no members of Georgia's delegation to the U.S. Congress in 1866 were allowed to take their seats. Instead, the Reconstruction Act, submitted by Radical Republicans, divided the South into five military districts. Georgia became part of the Third District, which included Alabama and Florida. Approximately fifteen thousand Federal troops were already stationed in Georgia as early as June of 1865 to help restore order. In Rome, members of the Twenty-ninth Indiana Regiment, Company C, under the command of Captain Lafayette Kyes, patrolled the streets and maintained a Federal presence (the regiment had detachments in towns between Marietta and Dalton).

General John Pope, of Second Bull Run fame, was appointed commander of the Third District. As directed by Congress, he registered eligible white and black voters to elect delegates to a new constitutional convention, which met at the end of 1867. This convention, which included thirty-seven African American delegates, abolished slavery for the second time and allowed blacks the right to vote. Interestingly, it also moved the state capital from Milledgeville to Atlanta, established the free public school system, gave women the right to own property and increased the governor's term to four years. In the elections of 1868, Republican Rufus Bullock defeated John B. Gordon, Democrat, by seven thousand votes and the new constitution was approved. For three years Bullock remained in office in an administration often considered to be the most corrupt in Georgia's history. Once the assembly approved the fourteenth and fifteenth amendments to the U.S. Constitution in 1870, Georgia was readmitted to the Union. In elections held at the end of the year, the Democratic Party was restored to power in Georgia. The Reconstruction came to an end.

THE FREEDMEN'S BUREAU

For the over five thousand freed slaves in Floyd County, the period between 1865 and 1871 was one of confusion, hope and ultimate disfranchisement. In March of 1865, before the end of the Civil War, Congress established the Bureau of Refugees, Freedmen and Abandoned Lands, known as the Freedmen's Bureau, to be headed by General Oliver Otis Howard of Maine. Its main purpose was to provide aid to former slaves through education, healthcare and employment. In Rome, the Freedmen's Bureau office was set up at 530 Broad Street (now the location of the DeSoto Theatre). Unfortunately, the officer chosen to head the Bureau in Rome, Captain Charles A. de la Mesa of Brooklyn, New York, did much to make himself disliked by the white population. He hung a large U.S. flag in front of the Bureau and made those who passed by salute it. In May of 1867, he had several men arrested following a provocative pro-Confederate play held to raise money to replace pews in local churches that had been damaged by Federal soldiers during the war.

As the Bullock administration took office in 1868, a new force arose in the state. The Ku Klux Klan had as its goal the political defeat of the Republican Party and the maintenance of white supremacy. The Freedmen's Bureau agents in Georgia documented 336 cases of murder or assault with the intent to commit murder against freedmen in 1868. There is no doubt that some of this political intimidation occurred in Floyd County and that many prominent men of the county were members of the KKK. Roger Aycock, in his book *All Roads to Rome*, reports that Marion Smith, the daughter of Charles H. (Bill Arp) Smith, remembered once seeing his Klan robes laid out in his room and being hurried from the room by her mother. Smith, as Bill Arp, had this to say about the Freedmen's Bureau in an article published in the *Staunton Vindicator* of November 17, 1865:

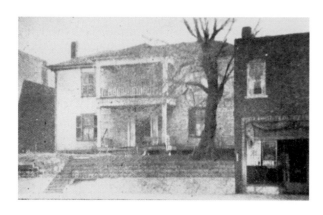

While not offering "forty acres and a mule," the Freedmen's Bureau in Rome, located at 530 Broad Street, did provide schooling and employment for the freed slaves of Floyd County after the Civil War.

They've give 'em a powerful site of freedom, and very little else. Nere's the big freedmen's buro, and the little buros all over the country, and the papers are full of grand orders, and special orders, and paragrafs, but I'll bet a possum some 'em steal my wood this winter or freezes to death. Freedman's buro! Freedman's humbug. I say. Jest when the corn neede plowin the worst the buro rung the bell and and tolled all the niggers to town, and the farmers lost the crops; and now the freedman is gettin cold and hungry, and wants to go back, and there aint nothin for 'em to go to. But freedom is a big thing—Hurraw for freedom's buro! Sweet land of liberty of thee I don't sing! But it's all right. I'm for freedom myself. Nobody wants any more slavery. If the abolishunists had let us alone we would have fixed it up right a long time ago, and we can fix it up now. The buro aint fixed it and it aint goin to.

When the Freedmen's Bureau closed its doors in 1872, its legacy included the creation of over one thousand schools for freedmen and their children in the South. In Georgia, over twenty thousand African Americans learned to read and write in the period between 1865 and 1872. However, this represented only 4 percent of the total African American population in the state. The return to power of the Southern Democrats in 1871 destroyed the dream of social and political equality for Georgians of color. Not until 1963, during what some historians call the "Second Reconstruction" of the civil rights movement, would another African American politician enter the Georgia Assembly as a member. (It is interesting to note that the population of Floyd County actually increased by 13 percent in the 1860s, despite the Civil War and hard times. The African American population declined by 3 percent during the same time period. In the 1870s, the population of the county increased 42 percent, while the African American population increased by a whopping 64 percent. This growth by both groups seems a sure indicator that the economy of the region had recovered some of its momentum despite a crushing nationwide recession in 1873. Land ownership by African Americans farmers, however, reached only 13 percent in 1900 in Georgia; most were forced to become sharecroppers.)

THE CLOCK TOWER

With its panoramic view of downtown Rome from atop one of the city's seven hills, the clock tower is the city's most historic and beloved landmark. It stands as a symbol of the rebirth of the city following the Civil War. Inside the ten-sided brick tower rests the 250,000-gallon iron water tank that, until 1960, served as Rome's water reservoir. Constructed in 1871 by Rome's Noble Foundry at the then-exorbitant cost of $49,000, the water tank, tower and adjoining pumping station addressed one of the city's pressing issues of the time: the need for a plentiful and fresh water supply for downtown Rome and the city's volunteer fire department. There was some opposition to the project; several citizens, including Daniel Mitchell, worried about the cost. One unnamed opponent of the project predicted that the tower's imposing height on one of the city's

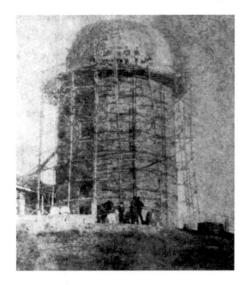

This faded photograph is the only known image of the construction of Rome's historic clock tower.

tallest hills would cause the water pressure to be so great as to "knock the bottom out of a tin cup!"

The bond issue actually failed in its first attempt at the end of 1870 but passed by a vote of 301 for to 146 against in February of 1871. Construction began soon after. The tank itself was built of ten-foot sheets of iron, manufactured at the Noble Foundry and then transported to Lowe's Hill (renamed Neely Hill, now Tower Hill), to be riveted together as a tank twenty-six feet in diameter and sixty-three feet deep. A three-foot space between the tank and the brick structure surrounding it provides for an interior spiral staircase of 107 steps.

In 1872, the clockworks and the bronze bell were incorporated into the wooden structure at the top of the 104-foot tower. The clockworks were made in 1872 by the E. Howard Clock Company of Waltham, Massachusetts, and shipped to Rome in October of that year on the order of John W. Noble. It needed to be wound once every eight days. The face of the clock is 9 feet in diameter, the minute hand is 4 feet, 3 inches and the hour hand is 3 feet, 6 inches. The bronze bell was a product of the Meneely Bell Foundry of West Troy, New York. It is 32 inches high and 40 inches in diameter.

Following construction of the tower and pumping station on Fourth Avenue, Dr. Robert Battey, the noted surgeon, remarked that he believed the water to be 100 percent pure and stated that the tower was a "large contributor to the success of his many surgical operations." Originally, a thirty-foot flagpole was installed on the tower. At its installation, the contractor discovered that he had forgotten to pull the cord through the pulley at the top. He offered five dollars to anyone who would climb the pole and pull the cord through. Sam Veale, then eleven years old, took up the task, for years afterward claiming the distinction of having risen higher than any other person in the city. In August of 1902, the wooden top of the tower caught on fire during an electrical storm. Firemen had to climb the steps and form a bucket brigade to put out the blaze.

Over the years, a number of renovations have been made to the clock tower, such as replacing the clock's original redwood hands with the current ones of yellow poplar.

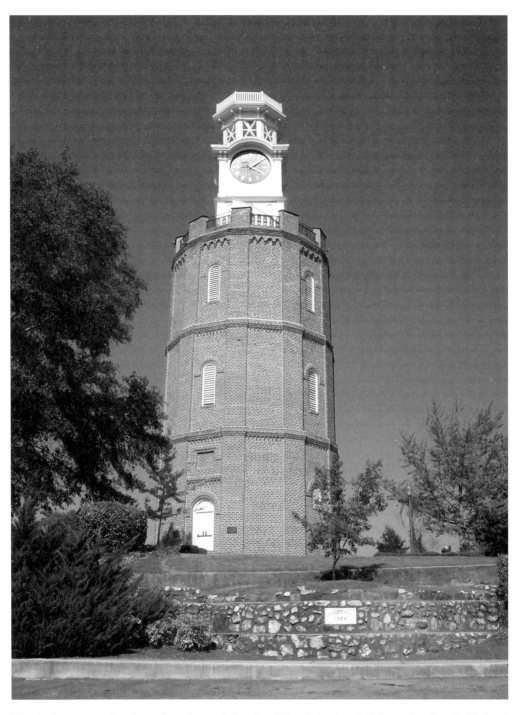

The clock tower stands today as Rome's most beloved and historic landmark. It is now listed on the National Register of Historic Places. *Photograph by the author.*

In 1953, the clock's original hand-wound mechanism was replaced with an electric one. In 1995, the Rome Jaycees raised funds to establish a museum inside the tower. The Clocktower Museum features a display of the original clockworks and life-size murals depicting scenes from Rome's history. It is now listed on the National Register of Historic Places.

EDIFICATION—PUBLIC SCHOOLS
AND SHORTER COLLEGE

The first schools in the region were the mission schools established by the American Baptist Committee on Foreign Missions in Cherokee lands in 1821. The Reverend Elijah Butler and his wife, Ester Butler, ran this school for the Cherokee near Coosa for eight years. Within twenty years of the founding of the city, several private schools had been established. The Cherokee Female Institute, established in 1845 as the Rome Female Academy by the Reverend and Mrs. J.M.M. Caldwell, was managed by Colonel Simpson Fouche in 1853. It passed into the possession of the Presbyterian church and became known as the Rome Female Institute, serving the community for many years, enrolling as many as 164 pupils in three departments: primary, preparatory and collegiate. Among its graduates in 1876 was Miss Ellen Lou Axson, later the wife of President Woodrow Wilson. The Rome City Directory of 1880 lists six private schools, including Professor Hiram Proctor's highly esteemed Select Male High School and the Rome Seminary for colored students.

The Directory of 1883 reported "the city (public) schools are to be organized September 1st, 1883 and will take the place of the public schools of the county, but will receive their portion of the school fund in addition to the amount voted by the city, which by special act, they allowed to levy a tax of ¼ of one percent, on real and personal property. The colored population share equally in this." The brevity of this report belies the fierce eight-year struggle by proponents of free public education in the city. As mentioned previously, the 1867 Georgia Constitution had a provision for the establishment of free public schools in the state. However, no state funds were to be appropriated; the assembly instead wished to authorize the establishment of free public schools in communities across the state that would provide their own funding. In addition, the assembly placed the restriction that two-thirds of the voting population in the community would need to approve the establishment of a local school system before a charter would be granted. Starting in 1875, the citizens of Rome began seriously debating the issue. Finally, in December of 1881, a citywide election was held. The measure failed by four votes.

After fifteen months of tireless work and promotion by community leaders, another election was held in May of 1883. This time the proposal passed by an overwhelming margin—87 percent of the voters approved of the establishment of a school system in the city. The city council wasted no time passing the necessary ordinances, establishing a Board of Trustees and donating a lot on Lowe's Hill next to the water tower. The cornerstone of the building was set in December of 1883. Ten months later, in October of 1884, the work was completed. The Board of Trustees rented a building on North Broad Street to serve as the first black school in the school district (in 1896, Main School, so called because it was the main school for black children in the city, was constructed on Watters Street in North Rome).

Benjamin Neely served as the first superintendent of Rome Public Schools. Born in 1834 in a small town near Baltimore, Maryland, Neely had run away from home at the age of thirteen after shoving his stepmother down a flight of stairs for striking his younger sister. Boarding a clipper merchant ship, he sailed as a crewmate for three years until by chance meeting a former neighbor in Dublin, Ireland, who convinced him to return home in 1850. He excelled in school, graduating from the College of Charleston in 1857 and taking a job as a schoolteacher at the Richmond Academy in Augusta, Georgia. During the Civil War, he served in Hampton's Brigade and became a Confederate spy (chosen because he "could speak like a Yankee"). Teaching history, Latin and French back in Augusta, Neely applied for the position in Rome and was immediately accepted by the Board of Trustees.

School formally opened on October 12, 1884; registration included 343 white students and 283 black students in grades one through seven (one through five in the black school). The Tower Hill School, later known as Central Grammar School, had six white female teachers. In his first yearly report in 1885, Superintendent Neely stated, "It is fair to say, that upon the whole, the first year's work of the Rome Public Schools has been, at least not a failure, and it is hoped that each succeeding year will add to the efficiency of the schools…your superintendent has not been idle, and your teachers have endeavored to do their duty." Following the superintendent's sudden death in 1892, the school was renamed the Neely School in his honor.

In 1873, the Cherokee Baptist Female College was chartered, the brainchild of Luther Rice Gwaltney, the pastor of the local Baptist church. A site for the new college was selected on Maiden Lane (Elm Street) on Shelton Hill (now Old Shorter Hill). An eight-room brick residence on the hill was purchased for $7,500. The school opened in October of 1873, Mrs. H.C. Cooper left her own successful private school to become principal and professor of English and history. Attendance the first year reached 124 students. Young women in the collegiate department studied the classics, music, science, art and drama. Following several down years, Alfred and Martha Shorter donated $20,000 to the college in 1877. Eventually the Shorters' additional donations, amounting to at least $200,000, helped to build three impressive buildings on the campus. The name was changed to Shorter Female College to honor their commitment to the education of females in the community.

The college flourished, gaining a reputation as one of the finest female colleges in the South. However, its location prevented it from expanding. In 1911, following donations by the Bass and Cooper families, the college moved to its present site in West Rome, the old campus becoming Rome High School. In the early 1950s, the Board of Trustees decided to accept male students and the name was changed for the final time to Shorter College.

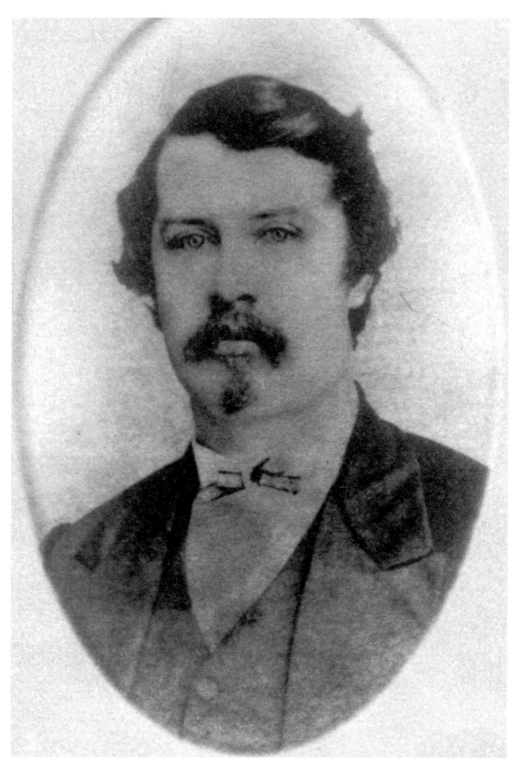

Benjamin Neely served as the first superintendent of Rome Public Schools in 1884. *Courtesy of the Neely family.*

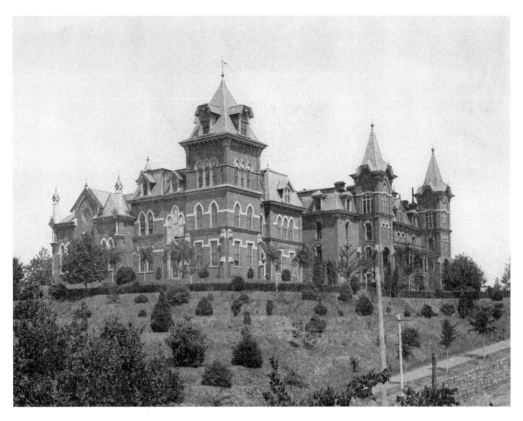

The original Shorter Female College became Rome High School in 1911.

VICTORIAN SPLENDOR— THE CLAREMONT HOUSE

Many fine homes have been built in Rome during its history. Arcadia, the home of Colonel Daniel S. Printup, built in 1850, is still noted for its unique design. Alhambra, the original home of Major Philip Walker Hemphill, is a beautiful example of the upper Georgia plantation-style, popular among wealthy planters of the period. Oakdale, a two-story Greek Revival brick building, was constructed near the banks of the Etowah River by John Johnson's slaves in 1853. Thornwood, a late Federal-style home, was built by Alfred Shorter in 1846. As the 1870s came to a close, a new suburban residential district developed in East Rome. Two fine examples of Victorian architecture were built in this district, one a brick house called Rio Vista and the other a wood house called Claremont.

Rio Vista, at 601 East Second Avenue, was built in 1879 by Colonel J. Lindsay Johnson, a newspaper publisher and textile mill operator. It had eighteen spacious rooms and soon became the social center of the city. Many famous people of the day stayed at the house, including William Jennings Bryan, presidential candidate in 1896, 1900 and 1908. Unfortunately, the home was torn down in 1958.

Built in 1882, Claremont House is one of the finest examples of Gothic, Second Empire Victorian architecture in the Southeast. The mansard roof is one of the most striking aspects of this period, adding height to the home and an air of mystery. The roof features a diamond pattern of red and gray slate tiles, as well as five different tile shapes. Peeking out of the roof are dormer windows. The Gothic arch over the front door, the shallow bay window, the cupola and turret are all classic elements of a Victorian home. Graceful curves embellish the woodwork on the façade. The decorated cornice is also highly representative of the style, also known as Renaissance Revival.

Colonel Hamilton and Florence Yancey began construction of the home in 1879. Colonel Yancey was a prominent lawyer in Rome, following in the steps of his father Benjamin Cudworth Yancey. The first structure on the land was actually the cottage, just behind the main house, built to appear as a miniature of the big house. Colonel Yancey and his wife lived in the small house with their four children for three years while the big house was built. In 1882, the family gratefully moved into their new spacious home. Eventually, the Yanceys had eight children and a series of servants who helped maintain the house and called Claremont home. The house was named in honor of a favorite cousin, Clare De Graffenried from Macon, Georgia.

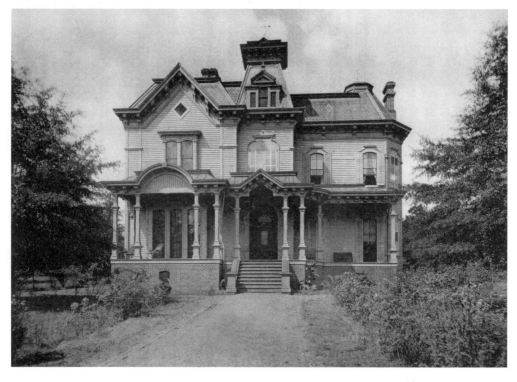

The Claremont House was built in 1882 by Colonel Hamilton Yancey and his wife, Florence. A fine example of the Second Empire style, the house today delights guests as a bed-and-breakfast.

The youngest son, Hamilton Jr., and his wife Nell inherited the home in the 1930s. As they did not have any children to pass it on to, in the 1960s the home changed hands. Charlie and Marion Shaw began the truly heroic task of bringing the home up to modern standards. Their greatest feats include creating the modern kitchen, finishing the upstairs floors, painting the exterior of the home and adding central heat and air conditioning. Marion Shaw selected the current delightful blue that so many admire. The Shaws actually painted it light green first and distinctly recall that they used 105 gallons of paint. The house was originally painted a gray color. In 1981, the Shaws received several awards from the Georgia Trust for Historic Preservation for their hard work in preserving the home.

In 1992, the Claremont House became a bed-and-breakfast. Tom and Patsy Priest added the sprinkler system along the top walls going throughout the house, a requirement by Floyd County for any bed-and-breakfast. To further comply with fire codes, a cedar closet was removed to allow better access to the servants' staircase as a fire escape. The Priests added an additional bathroom upstairs, giving each guest room a private bath. They refinished the wood floors, glazed claw foot tubs and completely reworked the plumbing. Today Holly and Chris McHagge are the innkeepers and guardians of this historic home on Second Avenue in East Rome.

The Hanging of Hayward Grant

For many years following the Civil War, July 4, Independence Day, came and went with little fanfare and sparse commemoration in the South. The city of Vicksburg, Mississippi, for example, did not celebrate the day until 1944, seventy-nine years after the end of the war. Romans did not take that long to recover their wounded pride or patriotism, eventually planning some events in 1879. The centennial year of 1876, however, saw the day pass solemnly, as the details of General Custer's defeat at Little Big Horn by the Sioux Indians a week earlier hit the newsstands. Ten days later, on July 14, the city trembled with an excitement equal to ten Independence Day celebrations. At eleven in the morning, the streets bustled with the biggest crowd in the city's history. Five thousand spectators braved an already hot summer's day to witness the first public execution by hanging in Floyd County in fifteen years.

From the founding of Georgia in 1733 until 1924, the legal method of execution was hanging. It is estimated that approximately five hundred legal executions occurred in Georgia during that time. The sheriff in the county or judicial circuit where the crime was committed was duty bound to carry out the sentence of the court, usually at a place within a mile of the courthouse. Until the 1890s, most states allowed public executions (the last fully public execution occurred in Owensboro, Kentucky, in 1936; since that time all executions have taken place within a wall or enclosure). During the eighteenth century, crimes for which the death penalty could be invoked were numerous, everything from petty theft to murder. However, by the middle of the nineteenth century, the number of capital offenses had been reduced. One crime that today does not often invoke the most serious penalty, arson, was a very serious offense 150 years ago, when almost every building in town was made of wood. A set fire had the potential to destroy an entire city. (Note: Much of the following is condensed from a news article written by Roger Aycock for the July 9, 1972 edition of the *Rome News-Tribune.*)

Late on the night of March 14, 1876, a store in Hillsboro (now South Rome) belonging to merchant J.B. Winslow burned to the ground. While investigating an earlier break-in at the home of Dr. John Kincaid on East Fourth Avenue, Detective Bud Taylor of the county sheriff's office found items, later identified by Winslow, in the possession of three suspects: George Wright (later found not guilty), Squire Looney and Haywood Grant. During the trials of Grant and Looney on May 30, it was determined that Grant had actually set the fire at the store to cover up the tracks of the burglary. Looney was found guilty of burglary at night and aiding an arson in a town and received a sentence of life in prison plus twenty years. The *Daily News* reported that on May 31, Judge John W. Underwood, unable due to intense emotion to read the finding and sentence of the court, passed the slip of paper to his clerk, A.E. Ross, who read the following:

> *Whereupon it is considered, ordered, and adjudged and sentenced by the court that you, Haywood Grant, shall be held in Floyd County jail until Friday, July 14, 1876, when on said day between the hours of 10 o'clock and 12 o'clock a.m. of said day, you shall, by said James M. Jenkins, sheriff, or his successor in office, be taken from said jail with a rope around your neck, to a gallows erected within one mile of the courthouse at Rome and that you be then and there, upon the said gallows, by the sheriff or his successor in office, be publicly hanged by the neck until you are dead, dead, dead, and may the Lord have mercy on your soul.*

For the next six weeks, the five newspapers in town reported almost daily on the life and times of Haywood Grant. Claiming to have been born in 1844 of free parents in Ohio, Grant, an African American, once belonged to General Bedford Forrest, who made his living as a slave trader before the Civil War. Sold "down the river," he worked on steamboats on the Mississippi until the Civil War, when he joined the Union army. Following emancipation, he undertook a life of crime, committing several robberies, and killed four men, including, he claimed, Confederate General Thomas C. Hindman in Arkansas (Hindman was killed by a shot through the window of his home by an unknown assassin in 1868).

The gallows were built on a vacant lot on Kingston Avenue in Forrestville (now North Rome), away from the center of Rome. Having been baptized the day before, Grant had a last meal of cornbread and mutton chops. He proceeded to the place of execution on a cart escorted by the Sheriff Jenkins, several deputies and four companies of the local militia. The crowd by then was huge, and all in attendance were searching for the best vantage points to view the spectacle. At the gallows, a member of the crowd accidentally caused the gun of one of the guards, George Benford, to discharge.

For a moment, pandemonium ensued, many thinking it an attempt to rescue the prisoner. When order was restored, Grant spoke a few words to Judge Underwood, who was much moved, and said goodbye to the crowd. At 11:20 a.m., the trap door opened. His neck was not broken, but he was pronounced dead six minutes later. Hanging for thirty minutes more, the body of Haywood Grant was cut down, put in a coffin and taken to Myrtle Hill Cemetery, where he was buried in ground set aside for criminals. The next day, the editor of the *Daily News* reported, "It was a mortifying sight to look upon, and we trust its like may never be seen in Floyd County again. The moral effect upon the people is not good. Death loses its terror in the excitement of the show, and the criminal is for a time a hero, if not a martyr." The last public hanging in Floyd County occurred in 1889, when Hardy Hamilton, convicted of murdering Chinese laundryman Joe Lee with an axe, was hanged near the Rome Railroad in Forrestville.

CHAPTER FIVE

A FRESHET IS A FLOOD

THE FLOOD OF 1886

Scientists now know that the eruption of an island volcano named Krakatoa changed the weather patterns of the world for five or six years. Located half a world away in the island chain of Indonesia, Krakatoa exploded in August of 1883 with the force of thirteen thousand Hiroshima atomic bombs, throwing twenty-five cubic kilometers of rock, ash and pumice into the atmosphere. The effect was startling. With all of these particles blocking the sun, the earth's temperature fell by as much as 2.5 degrees Fahrenheit. As the particles fell back to earth over the next six years, moisture collected on them, causing higher than normal amounts of rainfall (acid rain, as it turns out, since most of the ash was coated with sulfur dioxide). It also caused some of the most spectacular sunsets in world history.

By 1886, as the particles worked their way north of the equator, it became North America's turn to be hit by the Krakatoa effect. In March and April of that year, massive amounts of rain fell from California to the Maritime Provinces of Canada. Rains falling as fast as 3 inches per hour hit the West Coast, causing the Los Angeles River to flood, washing away every bridge. Continuing east, the rain then caused the Arizona Dam on the Salt River to collapse. The town of Santa Barbara, New Mexico, was wiped out by a flash flood, as was a church at La Joyita near the Rio Grande River. The original falls at Wichita Falls, Texas, were leveled by fast-moving waters. The storms then moved into the Southeast, causing flash floods and property damage. The Thomas, Jones and Company Foundry in Bibb County, Alabama, was totally destroyed. Floods were recorded in Macon, Georgia; Chattanooga, Tennessee; and Richmond, Virginia. The Ohio River crested at 55.8 inches above flood stage at Cincinnati, Ohio. Before hitting the Atlantic Ocean, the storms caused more damage in Pennsylvania, New York and New England. Montreal, Canada, had one of the worst floods in its history.

Situated on three rivers, Rome had experienced a flood or two just about every year of its existence. Known as "freshets," because they were most often an incremental, predictable rising of the rivers in the spring months, these floods were not particularly dangerous. Locals usually had plenty of time to move belongings to higher elevations.

These events were viewed only as a temporary annoyance. They even had a pleasant side effect, as the waters often smoothed the wagon ruts on the streets and cleaned off some of the debris.

In 1886, it started raining in Rome on Monday, March 29. By the following day, six inches of rain had fallen by noon and the rain continued. The Oostanaula River, always the first to crest, rose eight inches an hour as the waters quickly started moving up South Broad Street. A reporter from the *Atlanta Constitution* who happened to be in town wired the details of the afternoon of March 30 from the Western Union office at 223 Broad Street:

> *Early this morning the middle section of the new bridge of the Rome and Carrollton Railway washed away and is now lodged against the piers of the Broad Street bridge. Great fears are entertained for the latter bridge, and men are trying to remove the debris. Broad Street this afternoon presents a busy scene. Merchants are removing goods from their stores and taking every possible precaution against the flood...At the foot of Howard Street the residents are moving from one-story houses, and those residents in two-story buildings are moving upstairs.*

By the evening of March 30, the situation was more desperate as the unknown reporter kept to his post:

> *At this hour, 8:30 p.m., Broad Street from Norton's Corner to the bridge is one sheet of water from two to four feet deep. Every leading business house...is submerged. The cotton warehouse, water works, gas house, and a large number of private dwellings are under water. The flood is now within a few inches of that of 1881, which was the highest ever known in Rome, and the rivers are still rising eight inches an hour. It is raining in torrents. We do not know what tomorrow will bring forth. Intense excitement prevails and groups of people are on that part of Broad Street that is still dry....No loss of life is yet reported. The streets are in darkness.*

At 9:00 p.m., he made his last brave report:

> *The rivers are still rising. The water is nearly at the top of the tables in the Western Union office here, and communication can be held but a few minutes longer. The operator is telegraphing while standing on his table and momentarily looks for a break. Your correspondent has just returned from* _____ [at this point the wire connection was broken].

Early on the morning of March 31, the wooden covered bridge over the Etowah at the lower end of Broad Street gave way with a tremendous crash. Captain Luke Mitchell, the grandson of the founder, piloted the small steamer *Mitchell* up Broad Street in ten feet of water, turning west on Fourth Avenue to rescue citizens stranded on their homes in DeSoto. Several second-story windows on Broad Street were broken by the

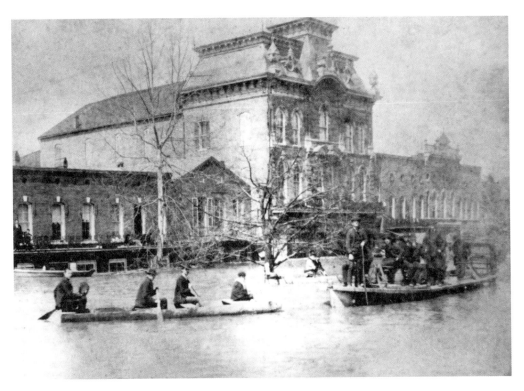

Men in rowboats and a small steamboat glide eight feet above Broad Street during the Great Flood of '86. The Nevin Opera House dominates the background.

waves caused by his passing. At least twenty houses were torn from their foundations, floating down the river, sometimes with the owners clinging to the roofs. A freight car overturned on South Street (First Avenue). Livestock, furniture, carts and buggies, lumber, store merchandise and the assorted contents of private homes were last seen on their way to Alabama.

By April 1 the rain had stopped. On the following day the waters, which had flooded to a record of 40.3 inches, started to recede. Romans began the process of digging out and cleaning up. Benjamin I. Hughes of the First National Bank reported that within a week, business was back to normal. Finding about $55,000 in paper currency totally soaked, not withstanding being protected by two layers of vault doors, the bank manager placed a large sheet of glass in front of a grate fire and individually dried each bill on the hot surface. Not a single dollar was lost. As a tribute to the spirit of its citizens, the city hosted a convention of Georgia Baptists a few days after the waters had receded (although there was still enough water to allow a few immersions if necessary).

The Second Avenue bridge was also lost, but soon an emergency ferry service was set up at the site. The Fifth Avenue bridge stood. Approximately $300,000 in damage was caused by the Great Flood of '86; only two lives, a mother and son, were reported lost. Additional high waters of at least thirty inches above flood level occurred in 1892, 1916, 1919–21, 1932 and 1936. In 1939, the H.H. Keel flood control levee was completed along the north bank of the Oostanaula River. Since that time, only a few "freshets" have temporarily covered the streets of the city.

THE NEVIN OPERA HOUSE

Prominent in many of the Flood of '86 photographs, the Nevin Opera House building dominated the landscape of Rome's Broad Street for almost forty years. Once called the "Madison Square Garden of the South," it had a seating capacity of one thousand, with standing room for two hundred more. It was built in 1880 by former Mayor Mitchell Albert Nevin and Mrs. Thomas H. Jonas for the sum of $21,000. The interior of the grand hall featured the latest gas lamps, tiered parquet seats and opera chairs, private boxes, opulent frescos and carved woodwork. The exterior of the four-story, Second Empire–style building featured an exquisite mansard roof with three round windows, a grand box office entrance and a side entrance stairway off an alley for stagehands and performers.

Many of the finest actors and musicians of the country performed at the Nevin Opera House. For a ticket price of twenty-five or fifty cents, depending on the seat location, a patron could see the great John Philip Sousa, the "March King," who appeared with his band in Rome at the opera house. Both the Boston Symphony Orchestra and the New York Symphony gave concerts at a music festival in 1898. Operas, plays, concerts, minstrel shows, operettas, political events and novelty shows all entertained Romans at 321 Broad Street. Productions featuring local musicians, such as the popular opera *Zelina*, were also performed on the stage.

Perhaps the grandest event in its history occurred in April of 1909. The one-hundred-piece Dresden Symphony Orchestra, founded by the great German composer Richard Wagner, on tour in the United States by special permission from Kaiser Wilhelm II, gave a performance of the Mendelssohn Violin Concerto in E Minor (and other compositions). Often considered by music historians to be the greatest collection of musicians ever brought to America, the Dresden Symphony Orchestra's performance was such a success that a later engagement in Chattanooga was canceled in favor of another appearance in Rome in May of 1909.

Following Nevin's death in 1895, ownership of the building changed several times. By the 1910s, the opera house began to show its age. In 1915, the city commission, on the recommendation of fire inspectors, closed its doors. The last performance in the building occurred in 1916, when a screening of the silent movie *The Birth of a Nation* was shown by special permission. On the morning of December 31, 1919, a fire began sometime between 3:15 and 3:45 a.m. By 5:00 a.m. firemen had the blaze under control, but the building was lost; damage to the nearby Woolworth Building and the Rome Supply Company was also extensive. Today, only Opera Alley remains as a reminder of the Nevin Opera House's grand cultural presence in Georgia's Rome.

One factor in the opera house's decline was the appearance of several movie theaters in Rome. The first of these, the Dixie Theater at 207 Broad Street, opened in 1908. It was soon followed by the Bonita at 237 Broad Street and the Lyric at 319 Broad Street. Not much more than vacant rooms with folding chairs and bedsheet screens, these establishments showed the popular silent films of the time. In December of 1911, the Elite Theatre (pronounced Ee-lite) opened at 225 Broad Street. It featured a $3,500 pipe organ, seating for 550 people and cost a whopping $20,000 to build. Eventually remodeled in 1924, the Elite became the Rivoli Theater (tickets were ten cents for adults and five cents for children). In 1929, the first movie theater built for sound in the South, the DeSoto, opened with a showing of *The Rainbow Man*, with Broadway star Eddie Dowling.

The Rome Symphony Orchestra

The same year that the Nevin Opera House burned down, Mrs. Edith Lester Harbin, founder of the Rome Music Lovers Club and the Junior Music Club, created the first Junior Orchestra in Georgia. In 1921, this group combined with Paul Nixon's Symphonic Band to form the Rome Symphony Orchestra, the first symphony in the South. The first concert, held in the Carnegie Library's small music hall on May 11, 1922, featured Nixon conducting performances of the Overture to Weber's "De Freischultz" and a program of Strauss waltzes.

Born in 1890, it was evident at an early age that Paul Burris Nixon would become a talented musician. After graduating from high school, he organized the Lindale Band, leading that group until traveling to Germany to study the violoncello. Serving in World War I, he earned the Distinguished Service Cross for Bravery in France. Returning to lead the Lindale Band, he helped organize the Rome Symphony Orchestra and became its first conductor. Under his leadership, the orchestra flourished, giving two or three performances each year for several years. Nixon was also a talented composer, presenting several suites, included the popular "Goldilocks and the Three Bears" and "Scenes from the Dark Continent." In the May editorial of the Rome *News-Tribune*, W.A. Patton wrote, "Every city has its first citizen so named for some civic achievement, but Rome has a first citizen named for this artistic genius and it is Paul Nixon conductor of the Rome Symphony Orchestra and leader of the Lindale Band and leader of all things musical."

During World War II, the orchestra disbanded for some time and then was reorganized under the leadership of Helen Dean Rhodes, who conducted performances until her death in 1976. Chartered as a nonprofit organization in 1977, the orchestra was led by John Carruth until his retirement in 1995. In 1982, business manager Kate Rodwell and board member Nancy Weers organized the Rome Symphony Women's Association, an auxiliary to the Rome Symphony Board of Directors. This group of dedicated ladies has been an invaluable asset in the support of the orchestra. In 2008, membership was opened to all, men and women, and the name was changed to the Rome Symphony Auxiliary.

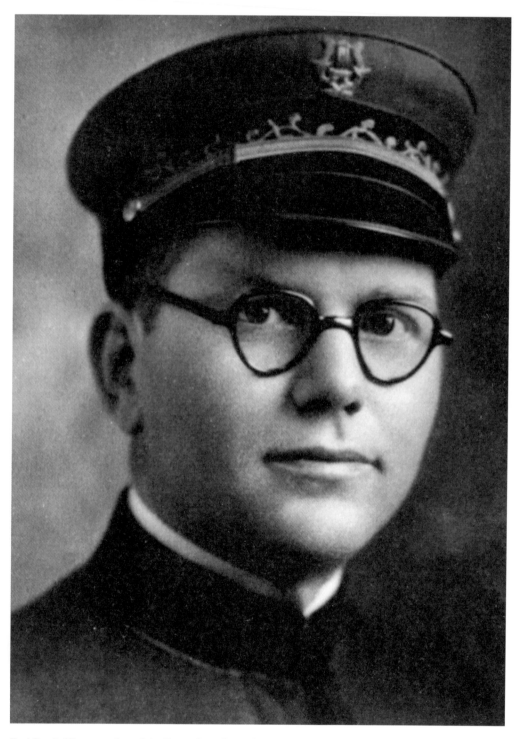

Paul Burris Nixon conducted the Rome Symphony Orchestra for many years during the 1920s and 1930s.

MOBLEY PARK

In an era before radio, television and the movies, Americans in the late nineteenth century looked for inexpensive ways to enjoy recreation time. The success of the amusement area at the World's Columbian Exposition, also known as the Chicago World's Fair, in 1893 led to the development of entertainment parks in cities across the country. The developers of the World's Fair had placed all of the rides, including the world's first Ferris wheel, and shows in a park-like setting. Over twenty-seven million people visited the park in the six months that it was open.

Now the campus of Darlington School, Mobley Park, later known as DeSoto Park, was located in South Rome on property once owned by founder Major Philip Hemphill. Samuel G. Mobley later owned the property, thus its name. Always a beautiful spot with a spring-fed lake, magnolia, oak and pecan trees and Alhambra, the stately former mansion of Major Hemphill, the area became a popular place for a picnic or leisurely boat ride.

In 1894, the five-acre property was bought by the City Electric Railway Company with one motive in mind—to make a profit. The scheme, modeled on the Chicago World's Fair only on a smaller scale, was masterfully simple: build a streetcar line from downtown Rome, charge people five cents to take the line to the park, charge them ten or twenty cents to enter a pavilion theater to watch performances, rent them boats, sell them ice cream at the Alhambra refreshment center and then charge them five cents to take the trolley back the three miles to town.

It was a great success. The Railway Company's manager, J.B. Marvin, soon found that he needed to run a fleet of eight cars, two every twenty minutes, to keep ahead of the crowds. A casino was built (later to become the Darlington School's first gymnasium) to present dramatic plays, amateur entertainments and dances. Arc lights were installed, along with a boathouse, colored lights at the pavilion, a baseball field, a small zoo, a row of swings, a bathhouse, a beautiful bridge and entryway and a driving range for horse racing. By 1911, the Rome Railway and Light Company had sixty employees running eighteen street cars to DeSoto Park (no one seems to know when the name change from Mobley Park occurred).

Then, for some reason, the park's popularity declined. One suspects that the automobile had something to do with it, Henry Ford having introduced the Model T in 1908. The city dweller and the country farmer were no longer limited by train schedules or distance to find new entertainments. By 1916, the park was sold to John Paul Cooper, who later donated it to become the grounds of the Darlington School. Still a beautiful spot, the sound of electric sparks on overhead cables and the smell of ozone no longer dominate the landscape, but as you walk along the southern end of the lake on the campus, you might still faintly hear echoes of laughter and fun from a period long ago.

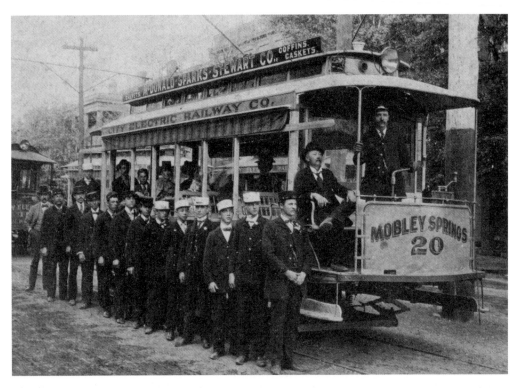

The City Electric Railway Company charged five cents to bring its patrons from downtown Rome to Mobley Park. The company had both open-air and closed cars.

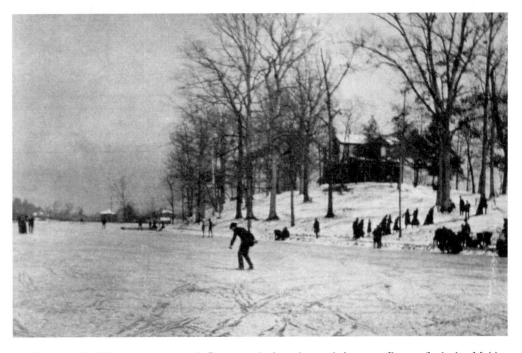

On February 13, 1899, the temperature in Rome reached ten degrees below zero. Patrons flocked to Mobley Park for a rare attempt at ice skating.

Volunteer Fire and Police

In ancient Rome, in AD 6 the emperor Caesar Augustus levied a tax on the sale of slaves to set up a new firefighting force. The members of this force were known as the Vigiles Urbani, or watchmen of the city. Dividing the city into districts, Augustus built barracks in each one for the Vigiles who patrolled the streets, especially at night, looking for unsupervised fires. They were equipped with pumps, axes, hooks, buckets, ladders, picks and mattocks (a small pickaxe). Each unit had its own medical personnel. As a public service, during down times, the Vigiles would visit private homes to ensure that they had adequate firefighting equipment, including a supply of water available in upper rooms, and proper exits in all buildings. In addition to firefighting duties, the Vigiles also served as the nighttime police force of the city, arresting thieves and robbers and catching runaway slaves.

Not much had changed by the end of the nineteenth century in Georgia's Rome. The first volunteer fire department in Rome, the Oostanaula Fire Company, Number One, of the City of Rome, was formally incorporated by the General Assembly of the State of Georgia during the biennial session of 1851–52. By 1898, the city had been divided into three fire districts. Rainbow Fire Engine Company Number One was organized in 1863. Its station was located at 506 Broad Street. This company, under Captain George Ramey, had one two-hose wagon, two drivers, two horses and forty-five volunteers. Citizens Hook and Ladder Company Number One, under Captain W.J. Griffen, was also stationed at 506 Broad Street. This company had one truck, two horses, one driver, one tillerman and thirty-five volunteers. It was first organized in 1869. Mountain City Fire Company Number Two was located at city hall on West Fourth Avenue. Captain P.H. Vandiver had under his command a hose wagon, two horses, two drivers and forty-five volunteers. This company was chartered in 1868. Number Four Fire Company was brand-new in 1898. Located at South Broad and Butler, under the command of Captain C.F. Taylor, this company had one wagon, one horse, one driver and thirty-five volunteers. The fire department office was located at 217 Broad Street, with Chief W.J. Griffin.

Equipped with ladders, pumps, axes, hooks, buckets and picks, just as the ancient Romans were, these volunteers had one tool that had not been available to Caesar's men: a brand-new fire alarm telegraph system. Thirty-one street alarm boxes that could send a coded electronic location signal to each fire station were spread over the city. The City Directory of 1898 noted the "keys are left at [the] nearest houses to the boxes, and one with each policeman, and also with responsible citizens." It also reminded its readers that "a heavy penalty is by law inflicted upon anyone detected turning in a false alarm, or in any way tampering with the boxes or their appurtenances [a big word meaning 'right of way']."

A popular spectator sport of the era was the training contests conducted by the volunteers. In May of 1889, Rome hosted a regional firemen's competition. Teams from Cartersville, Cedartown, Calhoun, Gadsden and Anniston, Alabama, and Dalton entered the contests, with the Mountain City Fire Company Number Two winning the two-horse race and the Rome Hook and Ladder Company winning the hook and ladder race.

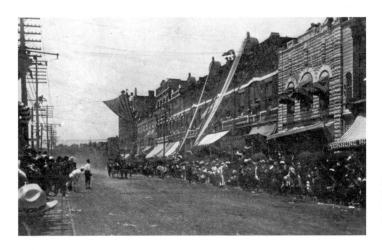

Crowds on Broad Street (some hanging from telephone poles) watch a firemen's competition in the 1890s.

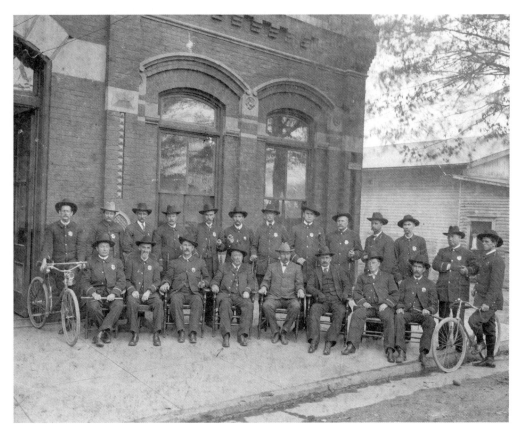

Chief of Police Horry Wimpee (seated fourth from left) posed with his men in front of city hall in 1889. Notice the bicycle patrolmen flanking the photograph.

In 1908, the Rome City Council decided to operate a paid, professional fire department. In 1911, the city purchased its first motorized vehicle, eventually becoming in a few years the second completely motorized fire department in the state of Georgia. Today, the Rome Fire Department consists of 153 full-time employees, including 1 fire chief, 2 deputy chiefs, 3 battalion chiefs, 2 secretaries, fire marshal and staff, chief of training and 1 master mechanic and assistant mechanic. The department operates under three battalions, working twenty-four on-/forty-eight off-duty hours.

Very little is known about law enforcement in the early days of Rome's history. The first Floyd County sheriff was Andrew H. Johnston, who began his service in March of 1833. Colonel William Smith served in that capacity for many years. Rome's first marshal was Sam Stewart. Nathan Yarbrough took the office in 1866, followed by T.G. Watters in 1871. In 1880, the City Directory placed police headquarters at 433 Broad Street. City Marshal E.J. Magruder, with a $700-a-year salary, had five patrolmen under his command to protect the town, at a salary of $40 a month. By 1898, J.B. Shropshire was city marshal and the headquarters had shifted to city hall. The first Rome police officer killed in the line of duty was James P. Mooney on April 18, 1874. He is buried at Myrtle Hill Cemetery and is listed with seventeen others on individual granite markers at the Police Memorial at 5 Government Plaza.

Turning the Century

By 1900, Rome's population had reached 7,200. The city had five private colleges and schools, two public schools, sixteen white and eight colored churches, three hospitals (Rome Emergency Hospital, Battey's Infirmary and the Martha Battey Hospital), thirty-four incorporated companies, five railroads and four street railroads, eighteen secret organizations (including the United Confederate Veterans, the Oddfellows, the Knights of Pythias, the Masons and the American Legion of Honor), twelve blacksmiths, nine barbers, six coal dealers, eight dentists, thirteen dressmakers, fifty-three lawyers, seven newspapers (*Cherokee Messenger, Hustler-Commercial, Masonic Herald, Rome Courier, Rome Georgian, Rome Tribune* and the *Southern Argus*), twenty-one physicians and surgeons, nine saloons, ten shoemakers and three undertakers.

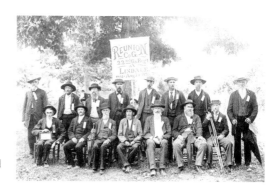

The survivors of Company G, Twenty-second Georgia Regiment, hold a reunion in 1895.

The city also had one band—the Mount Alto Brass Band—two bicycle shops, one carriage painter, two electricians, a florist, two harness makers, an ice manufacturer, two stove foundries, an umbrella repairer and one vinegar company. Within fifteen years, only the number of dentists remained the same. The twentieth century arrived and the only constant was change.

CHAPTER SIX

BOOM TOWN

COTTON IS KING

Cotton cultivation began simultaneously in India and South America at least five thousand years ago. Cotton cloth dating from 2,500 BC has been found in ruins in Peru and Arizona pueblos. In 425 BC, Herodotus, the Greek historian, described wild trees in India, "the fruit of which is a wool exceeding in beauty and goodness that of sheep." Although early explorers in North America reported finding wild cotton growing in the lowlands of the Mississippi River, seeds imported from the West Indies were first planted in the Jamestown Colony in Virginia in the 1620s. In Georgia, the crop was introduced soon after the founding of the colony in 1733. However, the labor-intensive crop did not really catch on, primarily due to the difficulty of removing seeds from the cotton boll. In 1791, the United States produced only four thousand bales (five hundred pounds each) of cotton, one thousand of which were produced in Georgia.

The invention of the cotton gin by Eli Whitney, a Massachusetts teacher/inventor, near Savannah in 1793 changed things completely. With the pesky problem of removing the seeds solved, Georgia's cotton production in 1796 increased to 21,000 bales. Over the next sixty years, the growth of cotton production in Georgia averaged about 10 percent per year. In 1860, just before the Civil War, Georgia's total cotton production reached 584,000 bales. Of course, the downside of this impressive growth was an equal expansion of slavery in the state. The vast majority of the 465,698 slaves reported in Georgia in 1860 worked the cotton fields. Following the war in 1865, Georgia's total agricultural production had dropped by 80 percent. The failure of the contract labor system and land reform instituted by the Freedmen's Bureau resulted in the development of a sharecropping system in the 1870s. With a predominately black workforce back in the field, cotton soon again became the king of Georgia's economy.

There has been some debate about how much of Floyd County's agricultural production was devoted to upland cotton. Although complete records are not available, it is safe to say that a substantial percentage of the acreage in the county grew the crop. In 1888, for example, in a special edition of the *Tribune*, it was noted that "Rome Territory" was responsible for an average 80,000 bales annually, producing 1,200 pounds to the acre. Simple math then shows that at least 33,000 acres of cotton were planted that year in the region.

However, Rome's major role in the cotton trade was one of collection and distribution. Its location on three rivers and the development of several railroads in the area resulted in the city becoming the cotton brokerage center of northwest Georgia. As early as two years following the first appearance of a steamboat on the Coosa River in 1845, Rome shipped twelve thousand bales of cotton to the outside world. Soon vast fortunes were being made in the cotton brokerage business.

The 1880 City Directory lists three cotton buyers and four cotton factors (commission merchants who sold crops for local farmers) doing business in the city. Located primarily at the foot of Broad Street between First and Second Avenues, in an area still called the "Cotton Block," these merchants brokered the buying, shipping and selling of cotton coming off the riverfront. By far the most successful of these men was Alabama native Theodore Howel. Coming to Rome in 1868 at the age of twenty-three, he entered the cotton business in 1873 with Captain J.J. Williams as his partner. Within a few years, the Howel Cotton Company was one of the biggest in the South, with additional offices in Tennessee, Arkansas and Alabama. His steam-powered, ninety-inch Morse cotton press could reduce the size of a standard bale of cotton by 67 percent, making it more water

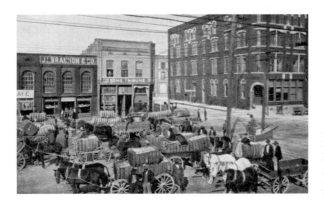

Farmers crowd Broad Street in the area known as the Cotton Block, awaiting buyers for their crop at the turn of the last century. The Rome *Tribune* building stands in the background.

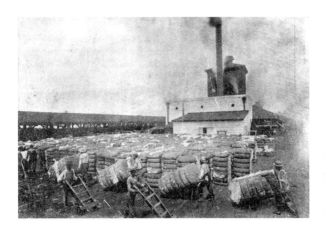

Workers stack cotton bales on the railroad platform behind the Howel Cotton Company warehouse. In 1888, 1,500 to 2,000 bales of cotton were being shipped from Rome each day.

resistant and easier to ship. Howel died in 1895, but his business continued until the 1910s (it is listed at 120 East First Street in the 1916 Directory).

In 1878, the Rome Cotton Exchange was organized. J.W. Rounsaville, a cotton factor in the city, was elected the first president. By then, cotton had made a complete recovery from the devastation of the Civil War. In 1880, Georgia had its first million-bale crop (proving, as one wit noted, that it was more profitable to hire labor than to own it). In October of 1887, the Great Piedmont Exposition was held in Atlanta (at which Henry Grady, formerly of Rome, introduced President Grover Cleveland to a crowd of fifty thousand) to promote better agricultural practices in the South. At the cotton competition, the first prize for the best bale of cotton went to a Floyd County grower.

By 1888, 1,500 to 2,000 bales of cotton were being shipped from Rome on a daily basis. This output soon attracted the attention of textile firms in New England looking to modernize their factories and searching for cheap labor. Why not build a mill in the South closer to the supply? Due to a concert of interests between city planners, businessmen and New South boosters, cotton and rayon mills soon became the leading industry in northwest Georgia, employing a large portion of the region's population.

By 1915, three cotton mills were located in the Rome area. The Massachusetts Mills Company at Lindale had six hundred employees running thirty thousand spindles and consuming forty thousand bales of cotton per year. Floyd Cotton Mills was a smaller operation located at East Eighth Avenue. On East Main and Cave Spring Streets, the Anchor Duck Mill began as a small operation in 1901 that produced cotton ducking, a heavy industrial cloth utilized for such things as awnings, tents, sails and ropes. Using ten thousand bales of cotton a year, the mill quickly created a boon for nearby cotton growers and supplied employment for hundreds of locals looking for work. Anchor Duck rapidly expanded its facilities and production after its initial debut in South Rome. By 1911, the working machinery included 178 looms and 14,000 spindles, up from a mere 24 looms ten years earlier.

Before the passage of the National Fair Labor Standards Act in 1938, child labor was used heavily in the textile industry: 20 percent of the textile workforce in the South was children under the age of sixteen. Children as young as eight years old worked ten- to twelve-hour days, six days a week, for about ten cents an hour.

Life outside of work orbited around the Anchor Duck community. Longtime mill manager D.D. Towers made sure Anchor Duck offered attractive amenities to entice workers to stay. Not only were there homes (although never enough of them to house every millworker), the community also had a company store, a meeting hall, a laundry, a barbershop and a school. Employees could find almost everything they needed without having to travel to the busy streets of downtown Rome. More than 150 houses lined the narrow streets of the village, making up different sections that eventually acquired unique place names over time, such as the Holler and Snake Island.

Life at the mill continued uninterrupted for nearly four decades. However, in 1947 Anchor Duck was purchased by the owners of Alabama Mills. Production was changed from cotton ducking to "novelty fabrics." The change in management led to a labor strike in 1948. Members of local 787 of the Textile Workers Union of America, complaining

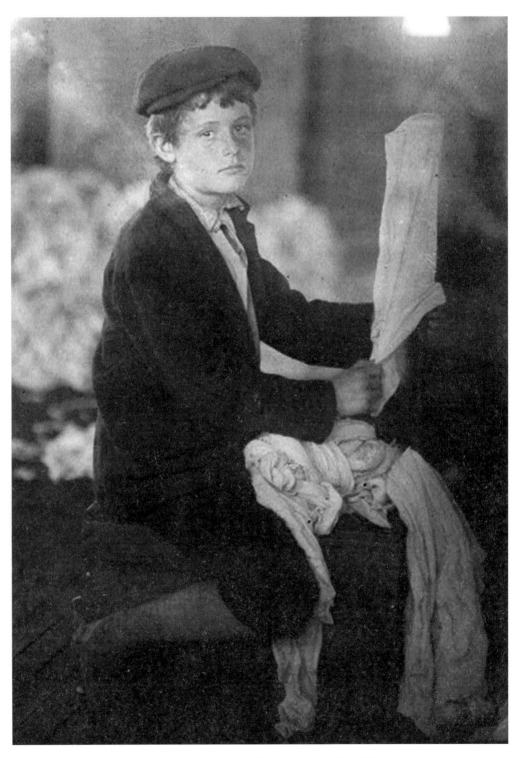

An unknown child works at the Cherokee Hosiery Mill in Rome in 1913. Children as young as eight years old worked ten to twelve hours a day for ten cents an hour until the passage of the National Fair Standards Labor Act in 1938. *Courtesy of the National Labor Committee Collection, Library of Congress.*

over "stretched out" work hours and management's refusal to recognize the union, walked out on March 19. During the summer and fall of 1948, several riots occurred between strikers and non-strikers, some ending in fatal violence. The year of the strike seemed to signal the beginning of the end. Although the mill continued production for several more years, it was eventually closed in the early 1950s.

In 1911, the cotton crop in Georgia peaked at 2.8 million bales. Then, on August 25, 1915, the first boll weevil observed in Georgia appeared in Thomasville. Reaching the United States in Texas in 1892, the approach of the boll weevil, cotton's greatest enemy, hung like Damocles's sword over Georgia agriculture. Nothing seemed to stop it. By 1919, losses were estimated at $40 million in Georgia alone. Cotton production plummeted. Without work, a mass migration began of white and black tenant farmers from Georgia to Northern cities, a trend that developed across the South. By 1957, production bottomed out at only 396,000 bales of cotton in the state. In 1987, a successful boll weevil eradication program was finally developed, leading to a revival in Georgia's cotton industry.

THE FAIRBANKS COMPANY

The oldest continuing manufacturing concern in the city is the Fairbanks Company, located on Division Street in West Rome. The plant has been in that location since 1887, although the company itself has an older history. In 1887, a small-scale company in Chattanooga relocated to Rome, changing its name from the Southern Scale Company to the Standard Scale Company. In the 1890s, the Fairbanks Company, a New England business with roots back to the 1820s (Thaddeus Fairbanks of Johnsbury, Vermont, invented the beam-type platform scale), purchased the company but retained its name until 1905, when it became the Rome Scale Company. When the parent company transferred the scale manufacturing operations to a new plant in Moline, Illinois, in 1907, another name change occurred. The Georgia Manufacturing Company began making two-wheel hand trucks and four-wheel platform trucks, along with wheelbarrows. Finally, in the early 1910s, the Rome plant became the Fairbanks Company.

During a period of expansion, the company added a line of swivel casters while dropping the wheelbarrow line and selling the scale rights to the Fairbanks Morse Company in 1927. The current operation in Rome includes a 9-acre lot with a 200,000-square-foot building. Employees use many of the same techniques for making their products as were used in the early 1900s, although more modern methods of heat treating, robotic welding, electrostatic coating and stamping metal have been adopted. During World War II, the demand for the company's products increased, resulting in a final expansion. Of particular note, the Fairbanks Company produced all of the hand trucks for the great ocean liners of the 1930s and 1940s, including the RMS *Queen Mary*, the SS *Normandie* and the SS *United States*.

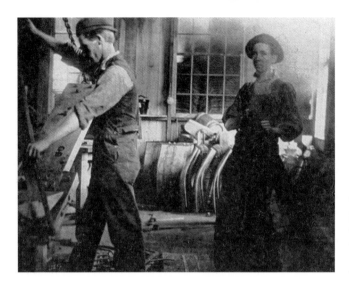

Workers at the Fairbanks Company have made hand trucks and swivel casters for over 120 years. It is the oldest industrial business in Rome. *Courtesy of the Fairbanks Company Archives.*

THE COCA-COLA STORY IN ROME

John Stith Pemberton, the creator of Coca-Cola, lived in Rome with his parents for most of his early life. His father ran a boardinghouse on Seventh Avenue. Moving to Atlanta to become a druggist, he invented the carbonated beverage in 1886 and sold it as a fountain drink. Before his death, Pemberton sold the rights to make Coca-Cola to Asa Candler in 1888. Candler, not believing that the quality of the product could be maintained in bottles, sold the bottling rights in the United States to two Chattanooga businessmen, Benjamin Thomas and Joseph Whitehead, in 1899 for one dollar, reserving the right to make and sell the syrup.

Thomas, Whitehead and a third partner, John Lupton, not having the capital to start a great number of bottling plants, soon began selling franchise rights to bottle Coca-Cola in areas across the country. Here the story turns full circle. Franklin Smith Barron was born in Carrolton sometime in the early 1870s. He was listed as a grocer in partnership with Tom Cordle at 309 West Fifth Avenue in the 1895 City Directory. Family tradition states that he twice went broke in the grocery store business. On January 10, 1901, Barron purchased the Coca-Cola franchise for Rome from Lupton and Whitehead for $250. Lupton and Whitehead received 5 percent of the stock in the company, expecting regular dividends. It became the sixth franchise in Coca-Cola bottling history.

By 1910, the company had become quite successful, operating out of 104–106 West Fifth Avenue. Competitors in the soft drink market in Rome at that time included the Floyd County Nova-Kola Bottling Company and the Royal Bottling and Manufacturing Company, sellers of a drink called Rye-Ola. The Cheery Nectar Company was organized in 1911, featuring a drink made with over forty ingredients. Boosters of the company proclaimed the beverage "is destined to become the most popular soft drink on the market and to make its proprietors millionaires, just as certain gentleman who organized another well known soft drink in Atlanta fifteen years ago."

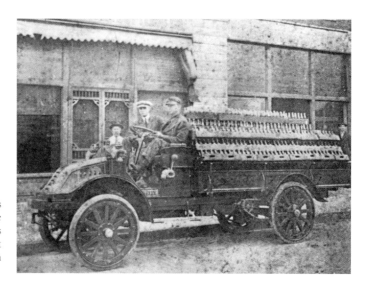

One of the early delivery trucks of the Coca-Cola franchise in Rome is loaded, in this photograph, with its product outside the bottling plant on West Fifth Avenue.

Following World War I, Barron's son, William Franklin Barron, joined the operation. Soon the company expanded into Carrollton, Cedartown, Cartersville and later Dalton, employing over two hundred people and operating over one hundred vehicles daily. By the 1950s, a third generation of Barrons began moving into the family business. William Franklin Barron Jr. (known as Frank), born in 1931, worked in the bottling plant as a child. Following the Korean War, he managed the Dalton and Cartersville plants. In 1976, construction was begun on a new bottling plant on Highway 27. However, changes in management and methods at the national level led the Barron family to sell their plant for $84 million in 1986. Today, although other bottlers have moved into the area, Rome is still considered to be a Coca-Cola town. Romans drink an average of 58.8 gallons of Coca-Cola products each year, making the city one of the highest per capita consumers of the product in the world.

THE STOVE CAPITOL OF THE SOUTH

At one time, Rome foundries produced more cast-iron stoves than any other city in the country except Cincinnati, Ohio. The availability of raw materials and the building of a pig iron furnace in the city contributed to the large number of foundries in the area. Originally known as the Rome Furnace, the smelting plant, coke ovens and other buildings were located on a thirty-acre tract of land on what became known as the Old Furnace Road (now Darlington Drive), south of the city proper. Reorganized in 1909 by R.G. Peters, an industrialist from Michigan, it became known as the Silver Creek Furnace.

It developed into one of the largest iron furnaces in the South. About one hundred employees turned the iron ore, mainly hematite mined near Cave Spring, into ingots of pig iron. The traditional shape of the molds used for these ingots was a branching

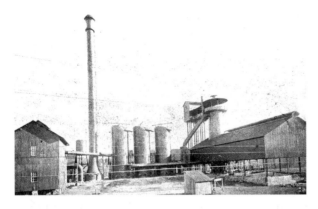

Left: The Silver Creek Furnace was one of the biggest iron furnaces in the South, producing eighty tons of pig iron each day.

Below: Rome produced more cast-iron stoves than any other city in the United States except Cincinnati, Ohio. *Rome Area History Museum Collection, photograph by the author.*

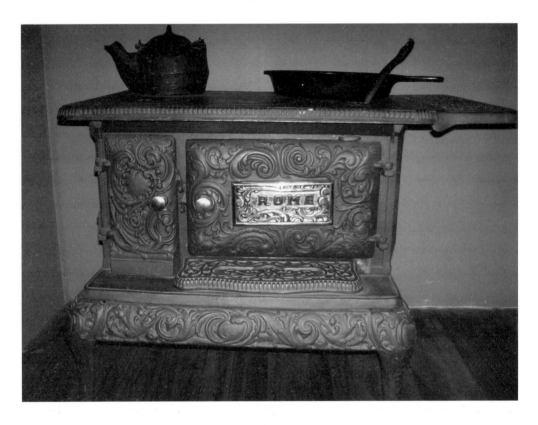

structure formed in sand, with many individual ingots at right angles to a central channel or runner. Such a configuration is similar in appearance to a litter of piglets suckling on a sow. When the metal had cooled and hardened, the smaller ingots (the pigs) were simply broken from the much thinner runner (the sow), hence the name "pig iron." The Silver Creek Furnace, at its peak, produced as much as eighty tons of pig iron a day.

The ingots were then transported to the foundry to be made into cast iron. Pig iron has a very high carbon content, making it quite brittle. To make cast iron, the pig iron is remelted in a small blast furnace. Scrap iron and scrap steel are added to increase the hardness of the mix and the carbon and silicon levels are reduced by a chemical process. Then the mix is ready to be cast in its final form, be it stoves, pans, kettles, railings, furniture or other utensils.

At least seven different foundries operated in Rome between the years 1882 and 1970: the Rome Stove Works, the Bowie Stove Company, the Eagle Stove Works, Rome Stove and Range Company, Southern Cooperative Foundry Company, Standard Stove and Range and Hanks Foundry. As the ore deposits petered out in Cave Spring and the area north of Rome to Summerville, other deposits in Alabama proved to be less rich and extensive. The Silver Creek Furnace closed. Many of the foundries continued, importing pig iron by rail. However, the demand for cast-iron stoves diminished after the introduction of rural electricity in the region during the 1930s. The last foundry closed in 1970.

"REMARKABLE ROME"

A promotional booklet of some length published by the *Rome Tribune-Herald* in 1911, entitled "Remarkable Rome," presented a summary of some of the other notable businesses in the city. O'Neill Manufacturing Company near Second Avenue, established in 1883, employed 100 workers to make sashes, doors, blinds, cornices, fittings, rails and other wood products for the interior of a house. The Towers and Sullivan Manufacturing Company employed 250 workers at its East Fourth Street plant. The company made steel and cast-iron plows, cotton planters, harrows, cultivators and a complete line of implement accessories. "Everything for the house from the foundation up" was the slogan of the Acme Lumber Company, which, notwithstanding a disastrous fire in 1911, employed 75 men in the lumber trade at its plant on North Broad Street. The Rome Furniture Company began in 1899 in North Rome. With a workforce of 100 men, the company produced $350,000 worth of oak furniture each year, specializing in bedroom and dining room suits and chifforobes.

In addition, the editors note the paving of county and city roads. By 1911, the county had paved two hundred miles of road, mostly using convict labor in the form of chain gangs. In the city, twelve blocks of the principal streets had been paved with vitrified brick (made with a process that makes the brick impervious to water) at a cost of over $225,000. Additional streets would be paved with asphalt macadam. Finally, after seventy-five years, the dirt streets and roads of the city would be, for the most part, mud free.

The booklet also sets forth the achievements and attributes of the city. Praising its climate, the editors note "the abounding rivers and the eternal mountains…temper the summer sun and the winter winds. No summer night is so warm that cover is not wanted. The average minimum winter temperature is 32.06 degrees above zero," amazingly just above freezing. Other qualities were expressed: "Rome's death rate is fifteen per thousand among the white people, one of the lowest in America. No malaria, but little fever or pneumonia and much old age." "Poultry Yards yield not only good dividends, but good health and wholesome pleasure." [Note: We have no idea what the last sentence means.] "There is a perfect system of sewerage." "Peace and good order prevail to a remarkable extent. Drunkenness and disorder are practically unknown. Crime records are at the minimum." "With great insurance companies, large banking resources, diversified industries and farming region surrounding, Rome is immune from hard times." And finally: "Rome is a happy, healthy, progressive city, the best place in the South in which to live and make a living."

CHAPTER SEVEN

FAME HAS A WING

From authors to admirals, from sports heroes to diplomats and pro wrestlers, Rome has been the birthplace or home of many individuals who went on to make an appearance on the national stage. Some made their mark by staying at home, while others carried the values and work ethic of their hometown to the far corners of the world.

HENRY GRADY, 1851–1889

Never was there a more tireless promoter of the South than Henry Woodfin Grady. As the managing editor of the *Atlanta Constitution* during the 1880s, Grady turned the newspaper into a platform for his "New South" vision. Born in Athens, Georgia, Grady was raised by his mother following his father's death at the siege of Petersburg during the Civil War. A graduate of the University of Georgia, he continued his studies briefly at the University of Virginia before returning to Georgia in 1869 to pursue a career in journalism.

Grady began his career covering what became known as "the Great Georgia Press Excursion" in 1869, a special train of dignitaries, reporters and businessmen, including Reconstruction Governor Bullock. The purpose of the trip was the promotion of Georgia's industrial potential. Grady, at the age of eighteen, found his way on the train, sending long and expensive telegraphic reports back to the *Atlanta Constitution*. Upon learning that his reports were heavily edited and cut to the bone, Grady found himself in Rome, Georgia, at 1:30 a.m. Sprinting from the railroad station, he discovered that the editor of the Rome *Courier*, Melville Dwinell, was still at his desk finishing the next day's edition. Dwinell, impressed by the young reporter's enthusiasm, stated that he still had a column open. Grady replied that he did not think one column would be enough. The readers in Rome woke up the next day to an extensive account of the press excursion, soon learning that the Rome *Courier* had hired a new associate editor.

Grady only stayed in Rome for about three years before moving back to Atlanta. For about a year, he learned all he could about the newspaper business from the venerable Dwinell, even while chafing at Dwinell's constant editing of his copy. In 1870, Grady and his younger

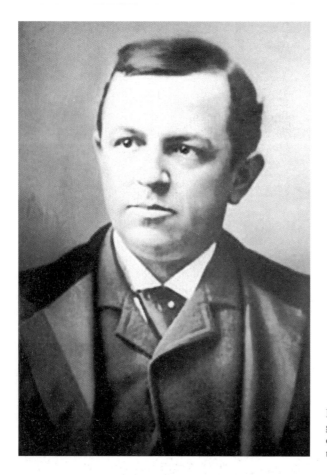

Henry Grady (1851–1889). One of the great newspaper editors and promoters of the "New South," Grady learned his trade while living in Rome.

brother Will became the editor and business manager of the Rome *Daily Commercial*. He married Julia King of Athens in 1871, and former college roommate Colonel Hamilton Yancy of Rome served as a groomsman at the wedding. While in Rome, his friend Joel Chandler Harris, the future author of the "Uncle Remus" folktales, visited often.

Finally, in 1872, hounded by creditors, Grady left Georgia's Rome. His promotion of the South as the part owner and editor of the *Atlanta Constitution* won him fame across the nation. His 1886 speech at a meeting of the New England Society in New York City (attended by J.P. Morgan and other investors) at Delmonico's Restaurant advocated a spirit of unity and trust between the North and the South. In this speech he proclaimed, "There was a South of slavery and secession—that South is dead. There is now a South of union and freedom—that South, thank God, is living, breathing, and growing every hour."

SAM JONES, 1847–1906

Although Cartersville, Georgia, rightly claims Sam Jones as its own, the fact of the matter is that Jones began his ministry and developed his powerful oratory right here in Rome.

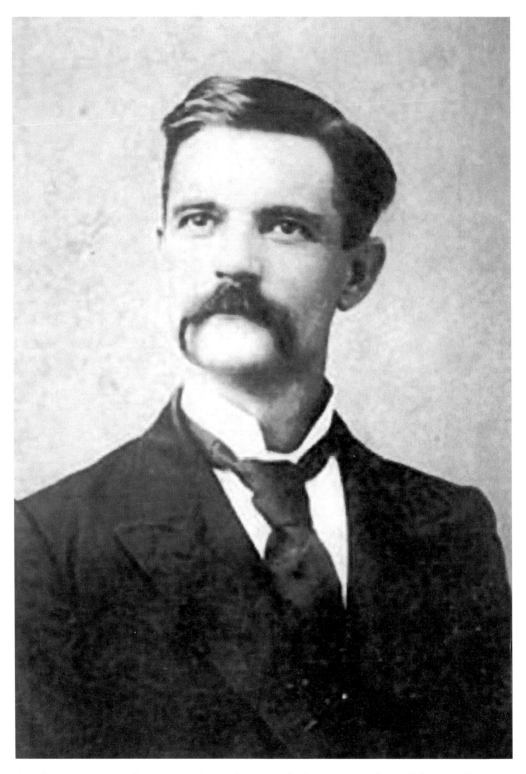

Sam Jones (1847–1906). Jones began his amazing evangelical career at the Second Methodist Church in Rome.

Samuel Porter Jones was born in Oak Bowery, Alabama, but moved to Cartersville at the age of eight, following his mother's death. He studied law and was admitted to the bar but lost his practice because of an extensive drinking problem. His alcoholism reduced him to a life of manual labor, working twelve-hour shifts at a local furnace for six years. A deathbed promise to his father to quit drinking and a religious awakening convinced him to enter the ministry.

Jones began his evangelistic career as a circuit preacher for the North Georgia Conference of the Methodist Episcopal Church, moving to Rome in 1875 to preach on the DeSoto Circuit as the pastor of the Second Methodist Church (now the Trinity Methodist Church). The new preacher quickly drove away some of the members of the congregation with his soul jolting delivery, but soon his fiery sermons began attracting large crowds. He particularly spoke against "demon rum," having as his target the dozen or so saloons on Broad Street. The conference, realizing that it had a star on its hands, appointed him as the fundraiser for the Methodist Orphan Home.

Moving back to Cartersville in 1877, Jones began supplimenting his income by conducting revivals across the South. In 1885, he converted Tom Ryman, a wealthy riverboat and saloon owner, in Nashville, Tennessee. Ryman built the Ryman Union Gospel Tabernacle in Nashville as a place where Jones could conduct his revivals (it eventually became the home of the Grand Ole Opry). It is estimated that he spoke to over three million people in 1885 and 1886, giving over one thousand sermons. Jones returned to Rome in 1897, where the overflow crowd at the Howel cotton warehouse was mesmerized by his talk entitled "Shams and the Genuine." He died suddenly in 1905 while on a revival trip. His body lay in state in the rotunda of the state capitol in Atlanta and then went on to Cartersville, where he is buried at the Oak Hill Cemetery.

VON ALBADE GAMMON, 1879–1897

Pedestrians on Roman sidewalks often stop at the corner of Fourth Avenue and Broad Street, next to the Old Masonic Temple building, to read two large cement plaques imbedded in the pavement. They tell the sad story of a young, talented life cut short and the brave mother who thus saved football in the state of Georgia. The total embodiment of a natural athelete, Von Gammon was good at everything—baseball, tennis, boxing, wrestling, running, swimming, bicycle racing, etc. His best sport, however, was football.

There are very few similarities between today's football and the football of the nineteenth century. Players wore very little protective equipment. Slugging and kicking were commanplace tactics. No substitutions were allowed unless a player was actually hurt. The game was much longer then, played in two forty-five-minute halves. The forward pass did not become "legal" until 1906, the most popular play being the "flying wedge." In this violent play, the team members locked arms in a V formation and ran as hard as they could into the other team's defensive line. Broken legs and arms were common occurances, and there was even an occasional death.

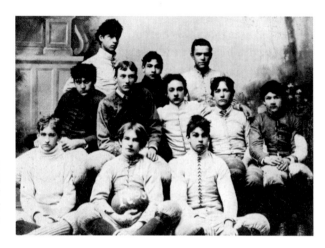

Von Gammon (1879–1897, pictured seated center with Rome Public School football teammates). A bill to outlaw football passed the Georgia Assembly following his death during a college game in 1897.

In 1896, Von Gammon graduated from high school and entered the University of Georgia as a freshman. Gammon became the quarterback on the football team, coached by Glenn Scobey "Pop" Warner, the man who later literally wrote the book on football strategy. In his sophomore year, a new player was added to the team, W. Reynolds Tichenor, who had played quarterback for Auburn the year before. Because Tichenor could only play quarterback, due to his size (at that time the quarterback only called for the hiking of the ball, which went directly to the fullback), Gammon, who was much more impressive physically, was moved to fullback. He quickly became the star player.

On October 30, 1897, the University of Virginia led the home team by a score of 11–4. As the second half began, Gammon was playing behind the line on defense. The Virginia wedge hit the Georgia players with a tremendous surge at left tackle. When the play was whistled dead and the players untangled, Gammon continued to lay on the ground, unconscious. Taken to the Grady hospital, he died eleven hours later of a fractured skull and brain concussion, his father having reached him before he perished. His mother arrived late to his deathbed. His funeral was held at the First Presbyterian Church in Rome, followed by his burial at the Myrtle Hill Cemetery.

Almost immediately, the Georgia Assembly passed a bill outlawing football in the state. It was sent to the desk of Governor William Y. Atkinson for his signature. He then received a letter from the grieving mother, Mrs. Rosalind Burns Gammon, asking him to veto the bill. In a letter to one of Floyd County's representatives she wrote, three days after her son's death:

> It would be the greatest favor to the family of Von Gammon if your influence could prevent his death from being used as an argument detrimental to the athletic cause and its advancement at the University. His love for his college and his interest in all manly sports, without which he deemed the highest type of manhood impossible, is well known by his classmates and friends, and it would be inexpressibly sad to have the cause he held so dear injured by his sacrifice. Grant me the right to request that my boy's death should not be used to defeat the most cherished object of his life.

Moved by her appeal, the governor vetoed the bill; football was saved. Twenty-seven years later, the surviving members of the Virginia football team presented a plaque to the University of Georgia in honor of Von Gammon and his brave mother. Unfortunately for the Gammons, tragedy again visited the family in 1900, when their younger son, William, following the first game of a baseball double-header in Cartersville, was struck and killed by a train.

MARTHA McCHESNEY BERRY, 1866–1942

Very few can match the impact made by Martha Berry on the educational landscape of Georgia. Born to comfort and upper-class late-Victorian respectability, she devoted her life to the education of the children of the poorer landowners and tenant farmers of the region. Her father, Thomas Berry, a Mexican War and Civil War veteran, operated a plantation, a grocery and a cotton brokerage business in Rome. When Martha was five, he moved his entire family (eventually including five girls, two boys and three cousins whose parents were deceased) to Charles "Bill Arp" Smith's former home, about two miles north of Rome. It later became known as Oak Hill (now restored as part of the Oak Hill and Martha Berry Museum complex). Educated by a governess and tutors, she also attended a finishing school in Baltimore, Maryland.

After her father's death in 1887, she assisted her mother in the family businesses and helped raise her younger sisters, ending an engagement with a promising young man from Virginia. Reaching the age of thirty in the mid-1890s, it seemed she had settled into a quiet, matronly life. Then one day, as the story goes, she was sitting in a small log cabin built as a playhouse on the family property that she liked to visit to read or write letters, when she saw three young boys looking into her window. She tempted them inside with apples and learned that they did not go to school or Sunday school. She read them a few Bible stories and invited them to come back the following Sunday. Soon dozens of young children were attending her impromptu Bible classes. Taking over an abandoned church at Possum Trot, she expanded the Sunday schools into day schools for poor children in the area.

In 1902, on eighty-three acres of land that had been given to her by her father, she opened the Boys' Industrial School, later known as the Mount Berry School for Boys. In 1909, she added the Martha Berry School for Girls. A tireless fundraiser, she used her connections to obtain additional land and money for the contruction of several more buildings. Philanthropists such as Andrew Carnegie and Henry Ford gave generously to support her vision.

She visited President Theodore Roosevelt in the White House, making him aware of the problem of rural education. On October 9, 1910, former President Roosevelt returned the favor, visiting the Berry schools on a rainy day. He toured the campus on a cart drawn by a pair of oxen accompanied by Martha Berry and his good friend Gifford Pinchot, former secretary of the interior. Teddy Roosevelt spoke for forty-five minutes at the School for Girls. A crowd estimated at 25,000 then heard another speech by the

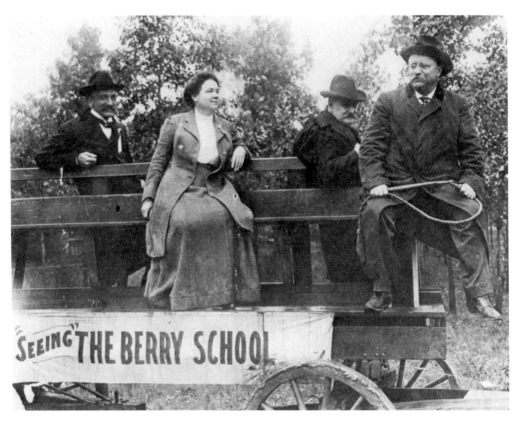

Martha Berry (1866–1942). Educator and philanthropist, she established day schools for poor children; these schools eventually became Berry College.

great man given from a special wooden stand supported by stacked cotton bales (large enough to hold 150 people) set up at Broad Street and Third Avenue (directly across from the current location of the Rome Area History Museum).

In 1926, Martha Berry established Berry Junior College, which in 1930 was expanded into a four-year institution. She died in 1942. Today Berry College is the largest landmass college in the world, over twenty-eight thousand acres including a sixteen-thousand-acre wildlife refuge managed by the Georgia Department of Natural Resources. A private, four-year accredited college with approximately two thousand undergraduate and graduate students, Berry College still has as its motto the words of Martha Berry: "Not to be ministered unto, but to minister."

ELLEN LOUISE AXSON WILSON, 1860–1914

Ellen Louise Axson was born in Savannah, Georgia, on May 15, 1860, to Samuel Edward and Margaret Hoyt Axson. At the age of six she moved with her family to Rome, Georgia, where her father had been called to pastor the First Presbyterian

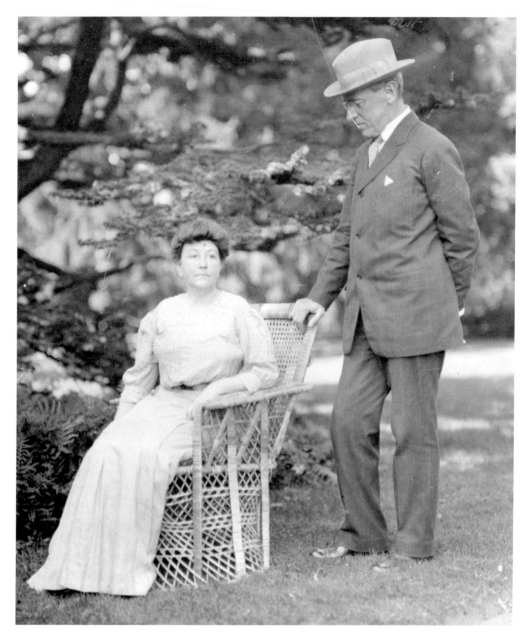

Ellen Wilson (1860–1914). She met her future husband, Woodrow Wilson, at her father's church in Rome. As first lady, she established the famous Rose Garden and fought for better working conditions for women.

Church. Graduating in 1876 from the Rome Female College, Ellen stayed at home to take care of her younger brother, sister and father. After the death of his wife in 1881, Ellen's father went into a deep depression.

While on a visit to Rome in the spring of 1883, a young Woodrow Wilson, who was staying at the J.W. Bones home at 205 East Tenth Street, attended church one Sunday and fell under the spell of the beautiful young woman who sat in front of him. He was even quoted as saying she had laughing eyes. After inquiring about her, his cousin arranged a picnic outing so the two could get to know each other. They met for the first time at the Brower home on Coral Avenue, where the picnic caravan of buggies and wagons left for a spring that flowed into Spring Creek, about eight or nine miles from Rome. The romance seemed to bud and only get stronger as the days passed, until Woodrow was called away to Johns Hopkins University.

After the death of her father in 1884, Ellen attended the Art League in New York, where her love of painting grew. Soon after, her schooling was finished and Woodrow obtained a teaching position at Bryn Mawr College for women. They were married on June 4, 1885, by her grandfather, Reverend I.S.K. Axson, and the groom's father, Dr. Joseph R. Wilson. They moved many times as Woodrow held several teaching jobs, eventually becoming president of Princeton University and then governor of New Jersey. In March of 1913, Woodrow Wilson was inaugurated as president of the United States.

Ellen used her position as first lady to make many changes that would affect people even today. Some of her most notable accomplishments included fighting for better working conditions for women and writing a bill that was passed on August 6, 1914, to better the living conditions for the slum areas around Washington, D.C. This was to be known as the Ellen Wilson Bill. Her personal touches can be found at the White House today in the famous Rose Garden, which she laid out, and the skylight that was put in her private painting studio. Twice a week, open house events were held. One of the days was always a Saturday so that working women could attend. In Rome, Mrs. Wilson set up a scholarship at Berry College for underprivileged and rural mountain children.

After a fall at the White House, her health started to fail and she was diagnosed with nephritis or Bright's disease, a disease of the kidneys. President Wilson stayed by her bedside until her death on August 6, 1914. On August 11, 1914, he returned with her body to Rome by train to be buried in the family lot at Myrtle Hill Cemetery. Services were held at the First Presbyterian Church. A funeral procession of buggies and people followed the horse-drawn hearse down Broad Street to the cemetery where she was laid to rest. In 2007, a ceremony was held on the anniversary of her death to rededicate her restored gravestone.

PRIVATE CHARLES W. GRAVES, "THE KNOWN SOLDIER," 1892–1918

Private Charles W. Graves of Rome, Georgia, was killed in action in France on October 5, 1918, during World War I. His name was chosen at random from the last shipment of war dead to return to the United States in 1922 to represent the "Known" American soldiers of that war. A nationally observed ceremony and parade in New York were held in his honor in tribute. In accordance with his mother's wishes, Graves was not buried next to the grave of the Unknown Soldier in Arlington Cemetery near Washington, D.C. His body was instead brought back to Rome and buried at the Antioch Cemetery on Callier Springs Road in early April of 1922.

However, following his mother's death, many Roman citizens, including Charles's brother, thought a burial in Myrtle Hill Cemetery would be a more appropriate honor. Others did not feel that his mother's wishes should be reversed. In April of 1923, the night before a court injunction preventing the moving of his body would go into effect, Charles's body was dug up by a group of citizens and moved to Myrtle Hill. He was buried for the third and final time. On November 11, 1923, in an impressive ceremony, thousands of civilians and ex-servicemen assembled at his gravesite to dedicate a marble slab memorial in his honor. In an event planned and coordinated by Rome's Shanklin-Attaway Post 5 of the American Legion, over two thousand schoolchildren placed flowers on the hero's grave.

The memorial was unveiled by the daughter of Almeron Walton Shanklin and the younger brother of Joseph Attaway. Lieutenant Almeron Walton Shanklin died as a result of machine gun fire at the Argonne Forest in October of 1918. Private William Joseph Attaway of the U.S. Marine Corps was killed by a machine gun bullet in June of 1918. As the first two of Rome's servicemen to be killed in action, the Shanklin-Attaway Post 5 of the American Legion was named in their memory in 1920.

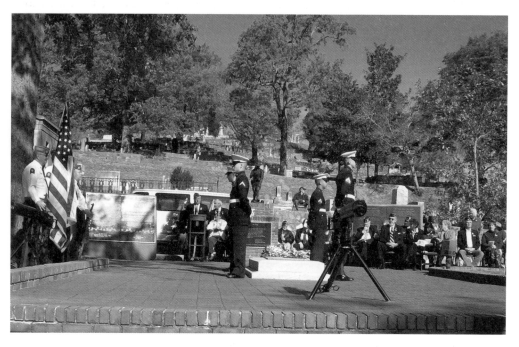

Tomb of Private Charles Graves (1892–1918). In the last shipment of American war dead from France, he was chosen to represent the "Known Soldier" of World War I. *Photograph of Veterans Day celebration at Myrtle Hill Cemetery, November 11, 2007, by the author.*

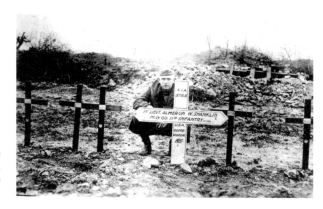

Lieutenant Robert Wyatt of Rome kneels at the grave of Almeron Shanklin of Rome, who was killed in the Argonne Forest in France in 1918.

ADMIRAL JOHN H. TOWERS, 1885–1955

In the history of the first one hundred years of aviation, John H. Towers stands tall as a fearless pioneer, a bold innovator and a true visionary. Widely regarded as the Father of Naval Aviation, Towers's name is inseparable from the development of naval aviation during the first half of the twentieth century. From the dawn of naval aviation in 1911 through the raising of the curtain on the Cold War in the late 1940s, Towers's willingness to experiment with new technologies, integrate them into the United States Navy and fight to win their acceptance by the navy, Congress and the American public are hallmarks of his long and distinguished career.

John Henry Towers was born in Rome, Georgia, on January 30, 1885, into a family with a proud tradition of military service. During the Civil War, his grandfather, Colonel John Towers, commanded General Robert E. Lee's Eighth Georgia Regiment in Virginia. His father, W.M. "Captain Billy" Towers, also fought under the Confederate flag as an officer in General Nathan Bedford Forrest's cavalry. Remembered as a studious and athletic boy, Towers learned to swim, dive and sail at an early age. It is said that by the time he was seven or eight, he was navigating the waters of the Oostanaula River in a small boat. After graduating from Rome High School in 1901, the future four-star admiral entered the United States Naval Academy, from which he graduated in 1906.

In 1911, Naval Aviator No. 3 Lieutenant Towers began flight instruction under the supervision of aviation pioneer and airplane designer Glenn H. Curtiss. Between 1911 and 1913, Towers set flight endurance records and took part in some of the first experiments in submarine spotting, bomb dropping, night flying, catapult launchings, aerial photography, airborne wireless radio transmission, scouting and reconnaissance. By 1914, Towers had become the navy's expert on aviation and its best flyer.

In July 1919, Towers played a major part in a milestone in aviation history when he organized and commanded the first transatlantic flight by three navy flying boats. After his own plane, the Navy-Curtiss NC-3, landed in stormy seas and was too damaged to take off again, Commander Towers and his crew improvised a sail and navigated to safety across two hundred miles of rough water. Only one of the three planes, the NC-4, successfully completed the flight. For his role in the expedition, Towers was awarded the Navy Cross.

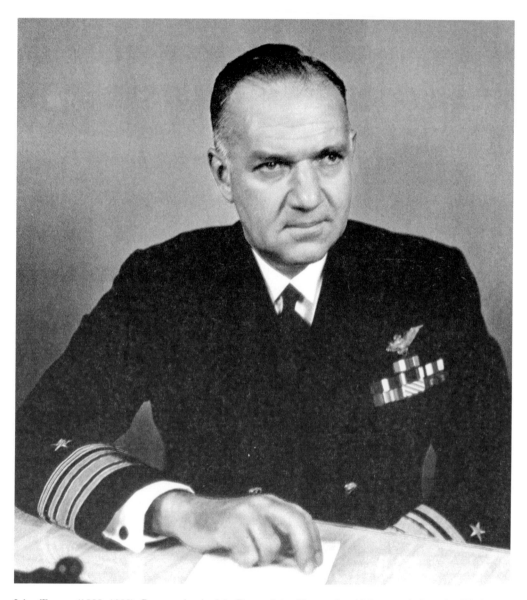

John Towers (1885–1955). Born and raised in Rome, John Towers is widely regarded as the "Father of Naval Aviation."

In September 1942, Towers was placed in command of the navy's air war against Japan. In charge of strategic and logistical planning, he played a key role in orchestrating victory in the Pacific, where the navy's aircraft carrier task forces spearheaded the action. Towers was appointed Fifth Fleet commander in 1945. In that official capacity, he was present on board the battleship *Missouri* to witness Japan's formal surrender on September 2, 1945.

HOMEGROWN

STAND WATIE was born near Rome on December 12, 1806. A leader of the Cherokee Nation, Watie was the brother of Elias Boudinot and the nephew of Major Ridge. As a member of the Ridge faction, he signed the Treaty of New Echota, which led to the Cherokee removal to Oklahoma. Escaping assassination, he became a successful plantation owner and served on the Cherokee Council. During the Civil War he became the only Native American general in the Confederate army. He was the last Confederate general to surrender in the field, ten weeks after the surrender of Robert E. Lee at Appomattox. In 1995, the U.S. Postal Service featured Watie on one of twenty Civil War commemorative stamps.

FRANK LEBBY STANTON was born in Charleston, South Carolina, in 1857. He came to Rome to become a reporter and then editor of the *Tribune of Rome*, living with his wife at the Wade Hoyt house behind Rome's City Auditorium. He later worked for the *Atlanta Constitution*. He became the first poet laureate of Georgia in 1925.

CHARLES FAHY was born in Rome on August 17, 1892. A graduate of Notre Dame University, Fahy was awarded the Navy Cross during World War I and returned to the states to practice law in Washington, D.C. Eighteen times he appeared as a lawyer before the U.S. Supreme Court, winning sixteen cases and being partially upheld in the other two. He was appointed solicitor-general of the United States by Franklin Roosevelt in 1941, advocating for workers' labor rights.

LEON CULBERSON was born in Halls, Georgia, in 1919, but lived for much of his life in Rome and is buried here. A baseball player in the textile leagues in the area, Culberson played center field for the Boston Red Sox between 1943 and 1948. He is best known for fielding Harry "the Hat" Walker's single in the seventh game of the 1946 World Series with Enos Slaughter on first base. Culberson threw the ball to the cutoff man, Johnny Pesky, who apparently hesitated before throwing late to catch Slaughter siding across home with the winning run for the St. Louis Cardinals.

CALDER WILLINGHAM was born in Atlanta in 1922, but grew up in Rome. A novelist and screenplay writer, Willingham is best known for his books *Eternal Fire* (1963) and *Ramblin Rose* (1972), both based in the South. He also wrote the screenplays *Little Big Man* (1970), *The Graduate* (1967, for which he received an Oscar nomination) and did some work for *The Bridge on the River Kwai* (1957).

WILLARD NIXON, born in 1928, lived most of his life in Floyd County. A graduate of Pepperell High School, he pitched for the Alabama Polytechnic Institute (later Auburn

University), setting a strikeout record that was not broken for thirty-nine years. Signing with the Red Sox, Nixon played for nine years in the Majors, where he was known especially for his mastery over the New York Yankees. After his career, he returned to Floyd County, becoming at one time the county chief of police. He died in 2000.

DAN REEVES was born in Rome in 1944. He quarterbacked the Dallas Cowboys professional football team for eight seasons and then became a coach with the team. He went on to become head coach in Denver (1981–92), New York (1993–96) and Atlanta (1997–2003). He still holds the record for the most appearances (nine) on the sidelines as either a player or coach in the Super Bowl championship game.

RAY CANUTE DONALDSON, pro football player, was born in Rome in 1958. Donaldson was selected by the Baltimore Colts out of the University of Georgia, where he was an All-Southeastern Conference selection. During his seventeen-year pro career he also played for the Seahawks (1993–94) and the Cowboys (1995–96). He earned a Super Bowl ring with Dallas in 1995

MARTIN ANTHONY LUNDE was born September 20, 1958, in Rome. Better known by his ring name, Arn Anderson is a former American professional wrestler, regarded by some professional wrestling experts as the greatest to never to have won a world title.

CHAPTER EIGHT

UNIQUE BECAUSE IT IS OURS

MYRTLE HILL CEMETERY

It is often described as one of the most unique and beautiful cemeteries in the South. More than twenty thousand of Rome's citizens (and a few Yankees) are buried in the thirty-two acres purchased from Colonel Alfred Shorter in 1857. Rome's first cemetery, Oak Hill Cemetery, was established in 1837 on Lumpkin Hill. However, the plot of land soon became too small and another high-elevation cemetery was needed. Located across the Etowah River in South Rome, the hill was covered with periwinkle, at that time often mistakenly called myrtle. It is also sometimes known as the "flower of death," because it is an invasive plant, appropriate then as a name for a cemetery.

The rural cemetery movement was a widespread cultural phenomenon in the mid-nineteenth century. It was inspired by romantic perceptions of nature, art, national identity and the melancholy theme of death. It drew upon innovations in burial ground design in England and France, most particularly Père Lachaise Cemetery in Paris, established in 1804 and developed according to an 1815 plan. Based on the model of Mount Auburn Cemetery, founded at Cambridge by leaders of the Massachusetts Horticultural Society in 1831, America's "rural" cemeteries typically were established around elevated view sites at the city outskirts. In fact, these cemeteries often became tourist attractions and places of recreation acclaimed for their beauty and usefulness to society.

Designed by Colonel Cunningham Pennington, a civil engineer, Myrtle Hill originally accepted interments at six different levels. Today the Broad Street entrance to the cemetery is dominated by Veteran's Plaza. The Tomb of the Known Soldier, Charles Graves, is guarded by three World War I Maxim machine guns and a bronze statue of a doughboy. Three thousand engraved bricks honor veterans and civilians for their service to this country. Also at the site are two monuments that once stood downtown on Broad Street. The Nathan Bedford Forrest Monument, erected by the Daughters of the Confederacy, honors General Forrest as the savior of Rome during Streight's raid in 1863. The Women of the Confederacy Monument is believed to be the first monument in the world to honor the role of women in war. The inscription on

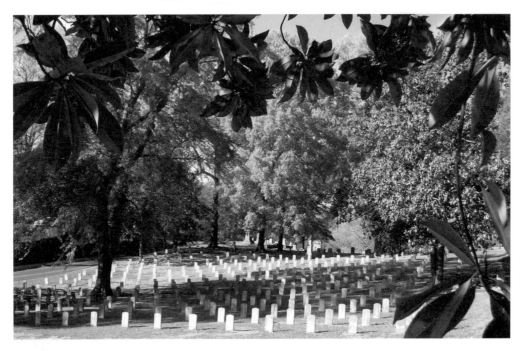

The Confederate section of Myrtle Hill Cemetery includes the graves of over three hundred Civil War soldiers, including two Yankees. *Photograph by the author.*

the monument was written by Woodrow Wilson, and the monument was dedicated in 1910 by Theodore Roosevelt.

One portion of the cemetery, known as the Confederate section, contains the graves of three hundred Civil War soldiers, including eighty-one unknown Confederate and two unknown Union soldiers. All of the eleven states of the Confederacy are represented in this section. Many of the notable early settlers, founders and prominent citizens are also buried at Myrtle Hill, including Daniel Mitchell, Dr. Robert Battey, Ellen Wilson, Colonel Alfred Shorter and Martha Berry's parents.

THE CAPITOLINE WOLF

Let's get one thing straight right at the beginning of this section. The bronze statue that sits outside the front entrance to Rome City Hall was not a gift to the City of Rome from Italian Dictator Benito Mussolini. It was a gift from the governor of Rome, Italy (the equivalent of our mayor), Francesco Boncompagni Ludovisi (1928–1935). Copies of the original, which is located in the Palazzo dei Conservatori on Capitoline Hill in Rome, Italy, are also found in Rome, New York; Cincinnati, Ohio; Brasilia, Brazil; and several places in Romania, Spain, Portugal and, for some unknown reason, Tajikistan.

The two small boys depicted on the statue are Romulus and Remus. Their tale has all the makings of a modern-day soap opera. The twins were sons of Rhea Silvia, daughter

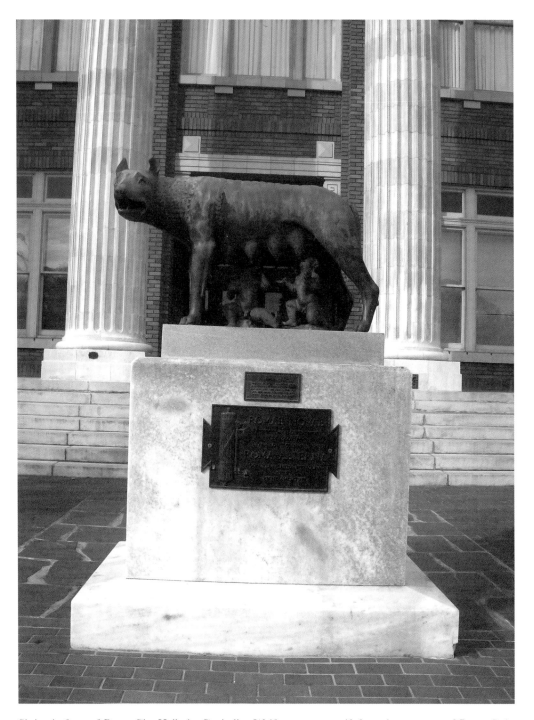

Sitting in front of Rome City Hall, the Capitoline Wolf statue was a gift from the governor of Rome, Italy, in 1929. *Photograph by the author.*

of King Numitor of Alba Longa, in the central part of Italy. When the king's brother, Amulius, overthrew him, he ordered Rhea Silvia to be buried alive and the twins to be cast into the Tiber River. However, the servant ordered to kill the twins could not, instead placing them in a basket and sending it adrift. They were rescued by a she-wolf (the Latin word for wolf, lupa, is also a Roman slang word for a low-class prostitute) who cared for them until a herdsman, Faustulus, found and raised them with his wife, Acca Larentia. The Roman historian Livy suggests that Acca Larentia had been a courtesan of immoral character before marrying Faustulus. Romulus and Remus grew and took revenge for the death of their grandfather and mother by killing King Amulius. The brothers then began plans for a city near the site of their rescue on the banks of the Tiber. During a quarrel over who should become king, Romulus killed Remus. He then built the walls of the city, giving it his name (or else our city today would be called Reme).

The original statue, it is thought, dates from about 500 BC. When the Chatillion Corporation Silk Mill of Milan, Italy, relocated to Rome, Georgia, in 1929, a full-size copy of the statue was presented to the city during the dictatorship of Benito Mussolini. Weighing three-quarters of a ton, the rather graphic depiction of the naked boys offended some people. During some civic events, the boys were even diapered and the wolf draped. In 1933, one of the twins was kidnapped and never found; a duplicate was shipped from Italy. During World War II, as Italy declared war on the United States in 1941, the statue was put into storage to protect it from vandalism. It was not restored to its place in front of city hall until 1952.

MASONIC TEMPLE

With elements of Gothic and French Revival architecture, the red brick Masonic temple, located at Broad Street and East Fourth Avenue in Rome, is second only to the clock tower as a recognized landmark in the city. Built in 1877, the first two floors and the fourth floor have held a variety of businesses and professional tenants. The third floor was the home of Cherokee Lodge No. 66, Free and Accepted Masons, for many years.

Freemasonry is a fraternal organization of obscure origins. It now exists in various forms all over the world, and has millions of members. The various forms all share moral ideals, which include, in most cases, a constitutional declaration of belief in a supreme being. The fraternity is administratively organized into grand lodges, each of which governs its own jurisdiction, which consists of subordinate lodges. The first lodge organized in Floyd County was Coosa Lodge No. 66, organized in 1848 with F.I. Sullivan as the first worshipful master. In 1855, it combined with Hunter Lodge No. 134 to form the Cherokee Lodge, with James M. Sumter as worshipful master. In 1876, the lodge purchased the corner lot at Broad and East Fourth Street. The building was built by A.J. Cooley, a local contractor who may also have built the Shorter College building at the same time in 1877. Today, the exterior of the building has been restored.

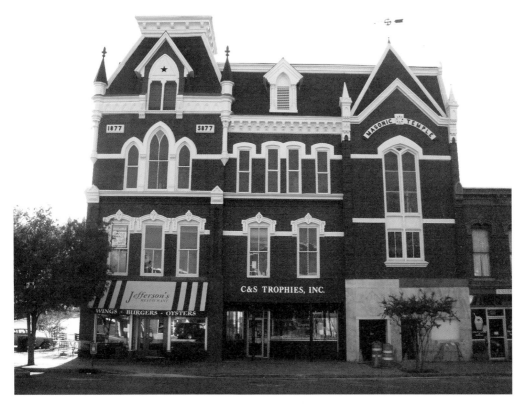

Rome's Masonic temple was built in 1877; the exterior was restored in 2007. *Photograph by the author.*

Perhaps the most illustrious of the Masonic members in Rome was Max Meyerhardt. Born in Prussia in 1845, he came to America at the age of four. Admitted to the bar in 1877, he practiced law in Rome, served as city attorney and judge of the City Court of Floyd County. His life was one of service for the betterment of his community. He became secretary of the school board and president of the Carnegie Library Association. As a Mason, he served as worshipful master of the Cherokee Lodge for thirty-nine years, master of the Seventh District Convention for twenty-six years and was grand master of Georgia Masonry for seven years. He established the *Masonic Herald* and served as editor. He founded the Masonic Home for Children in Macon. At his death in 1923, he was among the most revered of Masons in the entire country.

SARA HIGHTOWER LIBRARY

Between 1889 and 1929 over 2,500 libraries were built around the world with funds donated by industrialist Andrew Carnegie; twenty-four of them were in the state of Georgia. Today, while some have been demolished, many have been converted into museums, community centers, office buildings and residences. However, more than half

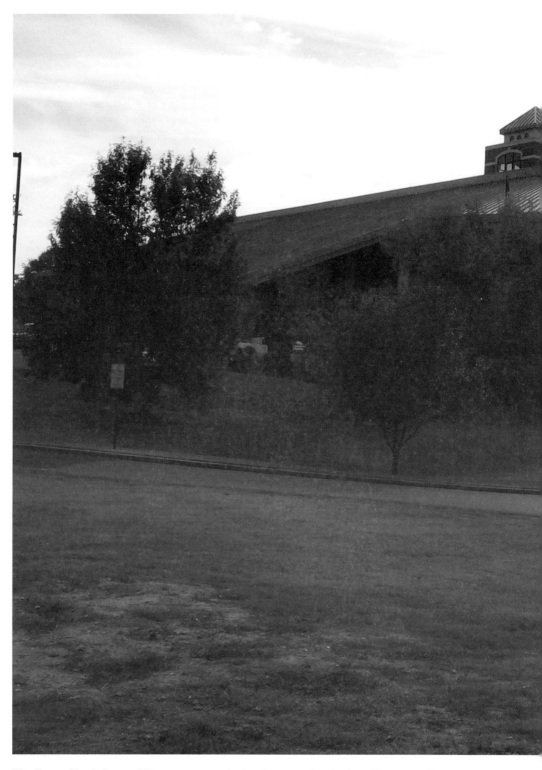

The Rome–Floyd County Library serves as the headquarters for the Sara Hightower Regional Library System. *Photograph by the author.*

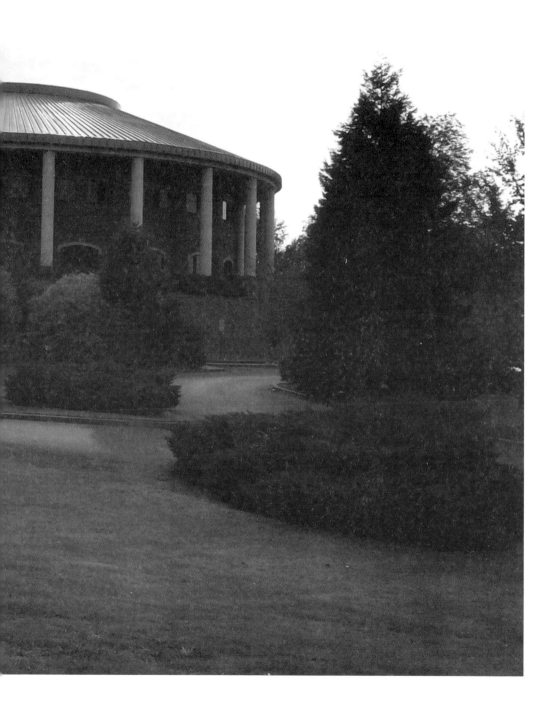

of those in the United States still serve their communities as libraries. In Rome, the Carnegie building, erected in 1911, now serves as office space for several of the city's government departments.

In 1988, a new seventy-five-thousand-square-foot library was completed on a seven-and-a-half-acre campus at Riverside Parkway near downtown Rome. The Rome–Floyd County Library serves as the headquarters for the Sara Hightower Regional Library System, which includes the Cave Spring Public Library, the Rockmart Public Library and the Cedartown Public Library. The library's website at www.romelibrary.org gives a brief biography of its namesake:

> *Sara Hightower was born on April 14, 1911, in Cedartown, Georgia. She received her BA degree from the teacher's college of the University of Georgia in 1928. She taught in Polk and Floyd County Schools and played an instrumental role in creating libraries throughout the Floyd County School system. After receiving her Masters of Library Science from Emory University in 1947, Sara initiated Bookmobile services in Floyd County while still overseeing the school library program for the county school system. She played an instrumental role in creating the Regional Library System that included Floyd, Polk, and Bartow counties. The Tri-County Regional Library System delivered books to citizens throughout the rural parts of Georgia. Sara Hightower's name became synonymous with public library services. Sara's services were recognized when she received the first Nix-Jones Award and was elected President of the Georgia Library Association in 1953.*
>
> *Even after retirement, Sara remained an active member of several library boards and her dedication was further recognized when a new Regional Library System consisting of Floyd and Polk counties was named the Sara Hightower Regional Library in 1980. Literally thousands of former school children and bookmobile patrons were on a first name basis with Sara. She is considered to be a true pioneer in bringing library services to all citizens of this area. When Sara died on April 8, 1991, the world lost one of those unique people who dedicated her life to serving others.*

ROME AREA HISTORY MUSEUM

As a vital center for local historical research, the Rome Area History Museum is appropriately located in the heart of historic downtown Rome at 305 Broad Street. Built sometime in the 1880s, the building has housed a furniture store, office space for local doctors and lawyers, a department store, an auto parts store and even a casket maker and embalmer. In 1996, the building was converted into a museum by local members of the Institute for Northwest Georgia History. Its purpose is to promote an understanding of our shared past, to enrich our lives and to inspire a stronger sense of community. The museum strives to achieve this goal through preserving, interpreting and exhibiting collections portraying the history of Rome and the surrounding area.

Thousands of visitors, young and old, have taken advantage of the programs and exhibits at the Rome Area History Museum. The permanent exhibits create a walk

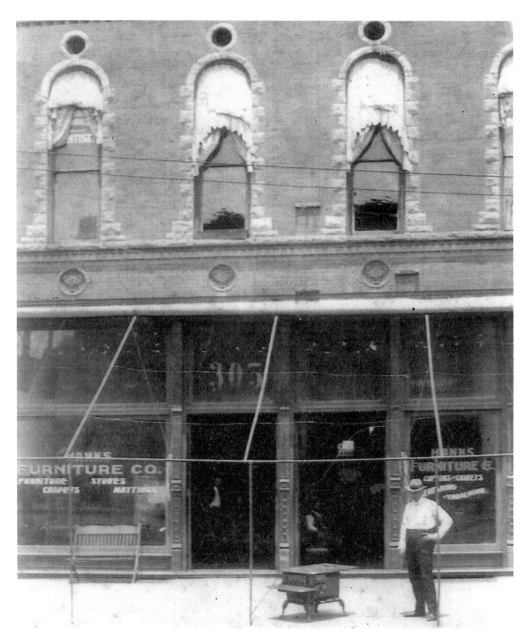

The Rome Area History Museum was established by local citizens in 1996. With a collection of over fourteen thousand items, the museum focuses on Rome, Floyd County and northwest Georgia history. Located at 305 Broad Street, at one time it was the location of Hank's Furniture Company.

through time, starting with the Native Americans and early settlers, through the Civil War and then the development of Rome's culture, life-ways and industries. Original documents such as maps, blueprints, photos, personal letters and business records provide primary sources that paint a picture of Rome's history. The archives house photographs, books, letters and manuscripts pertaining to Rome, Floyd County and northwest Georgia.

State Mutual Stadium

The original South Atlantic League, or "Sally League," ran as a minor league baseball league from 1904 to 1963, eventually becoming the AA Southern League in 1964. Many of the greatest baseball players in history played in the Sally League, including Hall of Famers Hank Aaron, Steve Carlton, Ty Cobb, Bob Gibson, Eddie Murray, Frank Robinson, Nolan Ryan and Willie Stargell. In 1980, the Single A Western Carolinas League brought back the Southern Atlantic League name. Currently, the Sally League has sixteen teams divided into two eight-team divisions. The Rome Braves, an affiliate of the Major League team the Atlanta Braves, play at State Mutual Stadium in the Southern Division with teams from Asheville, Augusta, Charleston, Columbus, Greenville, Kannapolis and Savannah.

Baseball had been a part of Rome's history for many years. The Northwest Georgia Textile League of the 1920s, '30s and '40s had several teams from Rome. A few of the players in this league even went on to play in the Major Leagues. However, the dream of professional baseball in Rome only became a reality in 2003. The Braves Single A affiliate had been in Sumter, South Carolina, between 1985 and 1990. Future stars David Justice, Jeff Bauser and Ryan Klesko played there. However, attendance only reached over thirty-six thousand fans once. The team never finished higher than third place. So in 1991, the Braves moved to Macon, Georgia, to play in sixty-year-old Luther Williams Field. By 2000, the Braves began looking for a newer park to put their Single A franchise.

In 2001, local citizens began seriously courting the Braves management. By 142 votes, or less than a 1 percent margin, the voters approved a special purpose local option sales tax, or SPLOST, to raise $15 million to build a stadium on Veteran's Memorial Highway. State Mutual Stadium construction began in the summer of 2002. It was completed in the spring of 2003, just in time for the Rome Braves' first home game on April 11. The stadium, built of brick to mimic the look of old textile factories, can accommodate 5,105 fans (plus room for more in a unique lawn seating area in right field), contains fourteen luxury boxes, state-of-the-art audiovisual technology, a full-service restaurant, six concession areas and a group pavilion.

The first year in Rome was quite successful, as 246,718 fans went through the turnstiles at the stadium. The team finished second in the Southern Division and won the Sally League Championship in the playoffs. Eight players on that team have gone on to play in the Major Leagues, including Jeff Francoeur, Brian McCann and Kyle Davies. Since

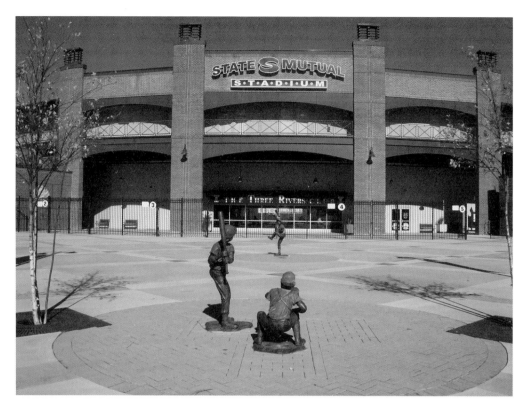

State Mutual Stadium has been home of the Rome Braves, a single A, minor league affiliate of the Atlanta Braves, since 2003. *Photograph by the author.*

that first season, the Rome Braves have not finished higher than third, but attendance continues to top 230,000 each year, adding to the quality of life in this small city.

A City on the Move

With populations approaching 36,000 and 100,000 respectively, Rome and Floyd County are experiencing rapid change. Positioned between Atlanta to the south, Chattanooga to the north and Birmingham to the west, its strategic location, affordable lifestyle and skilled workforce make it an attractive community for business. In 2007, the top employers in the county included several national names such as Mohawk Industries, Sara Lee, Pirelli Tire, Kellogg, Universal Tax Systems, Inland, Southeastern Mills and Suzuki.

Culturally, the city continues its fine tradition of bringing the arts to its citizens. The sixty-member Rome Symphony Orchestra, the oldest symphony in the South, under the leadership of Director Philip Rice presents six concerts each year. The Rome Little Theatre, located in the historic DeSoto Theatre, schedules a regular season of plays, musicals, dramas and youth programs. The Forum, Rome's civic center, located in the

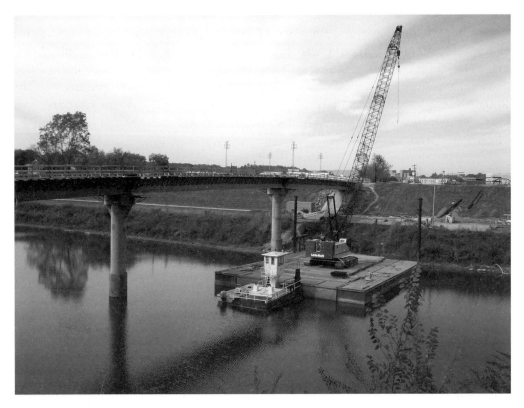

The walking bridge, under construction over the Oostanaula River, has a completion date of 2008. *Photograph by the author.*

heart of the historic downtown, hosts sporting events, concerts, business conventions and other family entertainments. The Chieftains Museum, originally the home of Cherokee leader Major Ridge, opened as a house museum in 1971, telling the story of the region's Native American inhabitants. The beautiful gardens, plantation house and museum at Oak Hill and the Martha Berry Museum interpret the history of Berry College and its founder. The Rome Area Council for the Arts strives to bring the best of visual and performing arts to the citizens of the region. The Rome International Film Festival, held each September since 2004, brings independent films and filmmakers from around the globe to the city. It is consistently rated as one of the best film festivals in the country. The Coosa River Nature Center at Lock and Dam Park and the Eubanks Museum and Gallery at Shorter College present a look at natural history.

Rome has four colleges—Berry College, Shorter College, Georgia Highlands College and Coosa Valley Technical College—and several healthcare facilities, including Floyd Medical Center, Redmond Regional Medical Center, Northwest Georgia Regional Hospital and the Harbin Clinic. The city is rated number one in healthcare of 193 small cities across the country. Three fine private schools complement the excellent city and county educational systems: Darlington School, St. Mary's Catholic School and Unity Christian School.

The Rome-Floyd Parks and Recreation Authority presents a variety of recreational choices. *Tennis Magazine* recently rated Rome as one of the "Top Ten Tennis Cities" in the United States. The authority also runs many youth and adult individual and team athletic programs, including soccer, basketball, softball and gymnastics. The Rome YMCA has additional recreation and life skills programs. A new city park, boat landing, interactive water fountain and walking bridge will soon be completed along the Oostanaula River.

The city's climate, notwithstanding the drought of 2007, continues to be moderate. The health and industry of its citizens is unmatched. Her society is cultured and educated. Her record of industrial and commercial success is steady and unfaltering. Rome continues to be a city on the move.

AFTERWORD

As George Battey suggested in his introduction to *A History of Rome and Floyd County*, much has been left out for another time. All omissions by accident or design are the responsibility of this author only. It would be fitting for the ancient Roman who started this work with a quote to end it with another. Pliny the Elder once said with great optimism, "From the end spring new beginnings." It would be tempting to stop there. However, a more contemporary Roman really deserves the last word, a few sentences to put it all into perspective. In the introduction to his book *All Roads to Rome*, Roger Aycock suggested that Rome's history "may be perhaps no more important or remarkable than that of any other community—but it is unique because it is ours."

Selected Bibliography

Abbott, Neil Suttles. *Within Our Bounds: A History of the Cherokee Presbytery, 1844–1974.* Rome, GA: Cherokee Presbytery, 1975.

Avery, Isaac W. *The History of the State of Georgia from 1850 to 1881.* New York: Brown & Derby, 1881.

Aycock, Roger. *All Roads to Rome.* Roswell, GA: W.H. Wolfe Associates, 1981.

———, Collection. Rome Area History Museum, Rome, GA.

Barron, Frank, Jr. *How About a Coke?* Rome, GA, 2001.

Battey, George Magruder, Jr., Collection. Special Collections, Rome–Floyd County Library, Rome, GA.

———. *A History of Rome and Floyd County, 1540–1922.* Atlanta: Webb & Vary Co., 1922.

Branham, Joel. *The Old Court House in Rome.* Privately published, 1921.

Byers, Tracy. *For the Glory of Young Manhood and Womanhood—Yesterday, Today and Tomorrow.* Mount Berry, GA: Berry Schools, 1963.

Candler, Allen D., ed. *The Confederate Records of the State of Georgia.* Vol. 1. Atlanta: Charles P. Byrd, State Printer, 1909–11.

Coleman, Kenneth, ed. *A History of Georgia.* Athens: The University of Georgia Press, 1977.

Cook, James F. *We Fly by Night: The History of Floyd College.* Rome, GA, 2006.

Cooper, Mark A., Collection. Special Collections, Rome–Floyd County Library, Rome, GA.

Dickey, Ouida, and Doyle Mathis. *Berry College, a History*. Athens: The University of Georgia Press, 2005.

Gardner, Robert G. *On the Hill: The Story of Shorter College*. Rome, GA: Shorter College, 1972.

————. *The Rome Baptist Church, 1835–1865*. Rome, GA: First Baptist Church, 1975.

Georgia Humanities Council and the University of Georgia Press. *The New Georgia Encyclopedia*. www.georgiaencyclopedia.org., 2004.

Goff, John H. "The Steamboat Period in Georgia." *Georgia Historical Quarterly* 12 (September 1928): 236–54.

Gregory, Chad. "Sam Jones: Masculine Prophet of God." *Georgia Historical Quarterly* 86 (Summer 2002): 231–52.

Harris, James Coffee. *Cave Spring and Van's Valley*. Cave Spring, GA: n.p., 1927.

The Heritage of Floyd County, Georgia, 1833–1999. Floyd County Heritage Book Committee, 1999.

Hudson, Charles M. *Knights of Spain, Warriors of the Sun: Hernando de Soto and the South's Ancient Chiefdoms*. Athens: University of Georgia Press, 1997.

————. *The Southeastern Indians*. Knoxville: University of Tennessee Press, 1976.

Jackson, Harvey H., III. *Rivers of Life: Life on the Coosa, Tallapoosa, Cahaba, and Alabama*. Tuscaloosa: University of Alabama Press, 1995.

Levin, Rose Esserman. *Voices in Protest*. Rome, GA: Rome Area History Museum Collection, 1988.

McElwee, Bobby G. *Images of America: Floyd County*. Charleston, SC: Arcadia Press, 1998.

Mooney, Burgett H., III, pub. *Past Times*. Rome, GA: News Publishing Company, August, 1989–2003, 2005–07.

Noble & Sons Iron Foundry Papers. Special Collections, Rome–Floyd County Library, Rome, GA.

Reynolds, Clark G. *Admiral John H. Towers: The Struggle for Naval Air Supremacy*. Annapolis, MD: Naval Institute Press, 1991.

———. "Confederate Romans and Bedford Forrest: The Civil War Roots of the Towers-Norton Family." *Georgia Historical Quarterly* 77 (Spring 1993): 20–40.

Roberts, Kate Quintard Noble. "A War Time Foundry." *Alabama Historical Quarterly* 18 (1956): 463–73.

Rome & Floyd County: An Illustrated History. Sesquicentennial Committee of the City of Rome, 1985.

Rome News-Tribune

Rome Tribune-Herald

Rome Weekly Courier

Saunders, Francis Wright. *Ellen Axson Wilson: First Lady Between Two Worlds*. Chapel Hill: The University of North Carolina Press, 1985.

Scott, Robin L. *Rome, Georgia in Vintage Postcards*. Charleston, SC: Arcadia Press, 2001.

Small, Marvin. "Steamboats on the Coosa." *Alabama Review* (1951): 183–94.

Towers, William M., III. *First Presbyterian Church, Rome, Georgia, 1833–1983*. Rome, GA: First Presbyterian Church, 1983.

U.S. Bureau of the Census. *Sixth, Seventh and Eighth Census of the United States: 1850, 1860, 1870*. Compendium.

Wilkinson, Warren, and Steven E. Woodworth. *A Scythe of Fire: A Civil War Story of the Eighth Georgia Infantry Regiment*. New York: Harper Collins Publishers, 2002.

Willett, Robert L. *The Lightning Mule Brigade: Abel Streight's 1863 Raid into Alabama*. Carmel, IN: Guild Press, 1999.

Wilson, Ellen Axson, Collection. Special Collections, Rome–Floyd County Library, Rome, GA.

Wright, Augustus R., Papers. Special Collections, Rome–Floyd County Library, Rome, Georgia.

Wyatt, C.J., Jr., Collection. Rome Area History Museum, Rome, GA.

———. *Upon This Rock, 150 Years in the Life of St. Peter's Church*. Rome, GA: Wallis Printing Company, 1994.